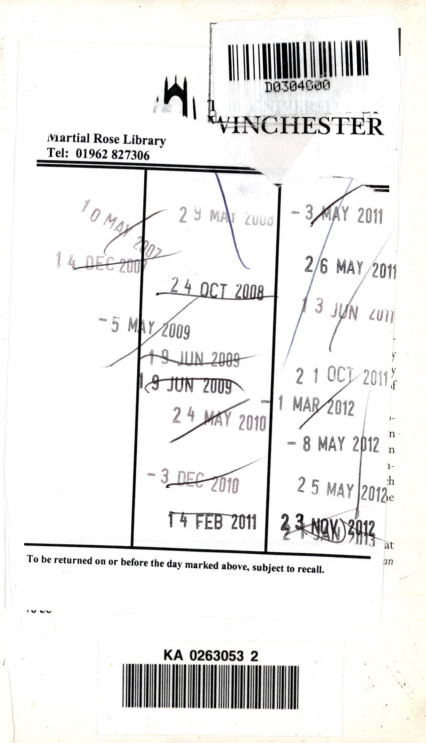

ROUTLEDGE CRITICAL THINKERS
essential guides for literary studies

Series Editor: Robert Eaglestone, Royal Holloway, University of London

Routledge Critical Thinkers is a series of accessible introductions to key figures in contemporary critical thought.

With a unique focus on historical and intellectual contexts, each volume examines a key theorist's:

- significance
- motivation
- key ideas and their sources
- impact on other thinkers

Concluding with extensively annotated guides to further reading, *Routledge Critical Thinkers* are the literature student's passport to today's most exciting critical thought.

Already available:
Jean Baudrillard by Richard J. Lane
Maurice Blanchot by Ullrich Haase and William Large
Gilles Deleuze by Claire Colebrook
Sigmund Freud by Pamela Thurschwell
Martin Heidegger by Timothy Clark
Fredric Jameson by Adam Roberts
Paul de Man by Martin McQuillan
Edward Said by Bill Ashcroft and Pal Ahluwalia

For further details on this series, see www.literature.routledge.com/rct

JUDITH BUTLER

Sara Salih

London and New York

First published 2002
by Routledge
11 New Fetter Lane, London EC4P 4EE

Simultaneously published in the USA and Canada
by Routledge
29 West 35th Street, New York, NY 10001

Routledge is an imprint of the Taylor & Francis Group

Typeset in Perpetua by Florence Production Ltd, Stoodleigh, Devon
Printed and bound in Great Britain by TJ International Ltd, Padstow, Cornwall

British Library Cataloguing in Publication Data
A catalogue record for this book is available from the British Library.

Library of Congress Cataloging in Publication Data
Salih, Sara
    Judith Butler / Sara Salih.
        p. cm.
    Includes bibliographical references and index.
    1. Butler, Judith. 2. Feminist theory. 3. Sex role. 4. Gender identity.
    5. Language and sex. I. Title.

HQ1190 .S23 2002
305.42′01–dc21   2001058587

ISBN 0–415–21518–8 (hbk)
ISBN 0–415–21519–6 (pbk)

CONTENTS

SERIES EDITOR'S PREFACE

The books in this series offer introductions to major critical thinkers who have influenced literary studies and the humanities. The *Routledge Critical Thinkers* series provides the books you can turn to first when a new name or concept appears in your studies.

Each book will equip you to approach a key thinker's original texts by explaining her or his key ideas, putting them into context and, perhaps most importantly, showing you why this thinker is considered to be significant. The emphasis is on concise, clearly written guides which do not presuppose a specialist knowledge. Although the focus is on particular figures, the series stresses that no critical thinker ever existed in a vacuum but, instead, emerged from a broader intellectual, cultural and social history. Finally, these books will act as a bridge between you and the thinker's original texts: not replacing them but rather complementing what she or he wrote.

These books are necessary for a number of reasons. In his 1997 autobiography, *Not Entitled*, the literary critic Frank Kermode wrote of a time in the 1960s:

> On beautiful summer lawns, young people lay together all night, recovering from their daytime exertions and listening to a troupe of Balinese musicians. Under their blankets or their sleeping bags, they would chat drowsily about the gurus of the time. . . . What they repeated was largely hearsay; hence my

lunchtime suggestion, quite impromptu, for a series of short, very cheap books
offering authoritative but intelligible introductions to such figures.

There is still a need for 'authoritative and intelligible introductions'.
But this series reflects a different world from the 1960s. New thinkers
have emerged and the reputations of others have risen and fallen, as
new research has developed. New methodologies and challenging
ideas have spread through the arts and humanities. The study of
literature is no longer – if it ever was – simply the study and evalu-
ation of poems, novels and plays. It is also the study of the ideas, issues
and difficulties which arise in any literary text and in its interpretation. Other arts and humanities subjects have changed in analogous
ways.

With these changes, new problems have emerged. The ideas and
issues behind these radical changes in the humanities are often
presented without reference to wider contexts or as theories which
you can simply 'add on' to the texts you read. Certainly, there's
nothing wrong with picking out selected ideas or using what comes to
hand – indeed, some thinkers have argued that this is, in fact, all we
can do. However, it is sometimes forgotten that each new idea comes
from the pattern and development of somebody's thought and it is
important to study the range and context of their ideas. Against theories 'floating in space', the *Routledge Critical Thinkers* series places key
thinkers and their ideas firmly back in their contexts.

More than this, these books reflect the need to go back to the
thinker's own texts and ideas. Every interpretation of an idea, even
the most seemingly innocent one, offers its own 'spin', implicitly or
explicitly. To read only books on a thinker, rather than texts by that
thinker, is to deny yourself a chance of making up your own mind.
Sometimes what makes a significant figure's work hard to approach is
not so much its style or content as the feeling of not knowing where to
start. The purpose of these books is to give you a 'way in' by offering
an accessible overview of a these thinkers' ideas and works and by guid-
ing your further reading, starting with each thinker's own texts. To use
a metaphor from the philosopher Ludwig Wittgenstein (1889–1951),
these books are ladders, to be thrown away after you have climbed to
the next level. Not only, then, do they equip you to approach new ideas,
but also they empower you, by leading you back to a theorist's own
texts and encouraging you to develop your own informed opinions.

Finally, these books are necessary because, just as intellectual needs have changed, the education systems around the world – the contexts in which introductory books are usually read – have changed radically, too. What was suitable for the minority higher education system of the 1960s is not suitable for the larger, wider, more diverse, high technology education systems of the twenty-first century. These changes call not just for new, up-to-date, introductions but new methods of presentation. The presentational aspects of *Routledge Critical Thinkers* have been developed with today's students in mind.

Each book in the series has a similar structure. They begin with a section offering an overview of the life and ideas of each thinker and explain why she or he is important. The central section of each book discusses the thinker's key ideas, their context, evolution and reception. Each book concludes with a survey of the thinker's impact, outlining how their ideas have been taken up and developed by others. In addition, there is a detailed final section suggesting and describing books for further reading. This is not a 'tacked-on' section but an integral part of each volume. In the first part of this section you will find brief descriptions of the thinker's key works, then, following this, information on the most useful critical works and, in some cases, on relevant web sites. This section will guide you in your reading, enabling you to follow your interests and develop your own projects. Throughout each book, references are given in what is known as the Harvard system (the author and the date of a work cited are given in the text and you can look up the full details in the bibliography at the back). This offers a lot of information in very little space. The books also explain technical terms and use boxes to describe events or ideas in more detail, away from the main emphasis of the discussion. Boxes are also used at times to highlight definitions of terms frequently used or coined by a thinker. In this way, the boxes serve as a kind of glossary, easily identified when flicking through the book.

The thinkers in the series are 'critical' for three reasons. First, they are examined in the light of subjects which involve criticism: principally literary studies or English and cultural studies, but also other disciplines which rely on the criticism of books, ideas, theories and unquestioned assumptions. Second, studying their work will provide you with a 'tool kit' for informed critical reading and thought, which will heighten your own criticism. Third, these thinkers are critical because they are crucially important: they deal with ideas and questions which can overturn conventional understandings of the world, of texts, of everything we take for granted, leaving us with a deeper understanding of what we already knew and with new ideas.

No introduction can tell you everything. However, by offering a way into critical thinking, this series hopes to begin to engage you in an activity which is productive, constructive and potentially life-changing.

ACKNOWLEDGEMENTS

Thanks are due to Robert Eaglestone for intelligent, incisive editing; to Liz Thompson at Routledge for her patience and ruthless cutting; to Rod Edmond at the University of Kent for good advice; and to Robert McGill, who read drafts, suggested changes, looked up references, and was generally very good-humoured about the whole thing.

ABBREVIATIONS

References to books, articles and interviews by Judith Butler are abbreviated in the text as below; publication details for these and other works by Butler appear in the Further Reading section. For references to works by other authors the Harvard system is used; full bibliographical details of these may be found in the Works Cited section.

BTM   *Bodies That Matter* (1993)
CF   'Contingent Foundations' (1990/2)
CHU   *Contingency, Hegemony, Universality* (2000)
CTS   'Changing the Subject' (2000)
ES   *Excitable Speech* (1997)
FPBI   'Foucault and the Paradox of Bodily Inscriptions' (1989)
GP   'Gender as Performance' (1994)
GT   *Gender Trouble* (first edition, 1990)
GTII   *Gender Trouble* (anniversary edition, 1999)
NTI   'The Nothing That Is' (1991)
PLP   *The Psychic Life of Power* (1997)
RBP   'Revisiting Bodies and Pleasures' (1999)
SD   *Subjects of Desire* (first edition, 1987)
SDII   *Subjects of Desire* (reprint, 1999)
SG   'Sex and Gender in Simone de Beauvoir's *Second Sex*' (1986)

SI	'Sexual Inversions' (1996)
VSG	'Variations on Sex and Gender' (1987)
WIC	'What Is Critique?' (2000)
WLT	*What's Left of Theory?* (2000)

WHY BUTLER?

If you were to approach someone working in the critical theoretical field with the question 'Who's Judith Butler?' their reply might contain the words 'queer theory', 'feminist theory' and 'gender studies'. Probe a little deeper, and you might hear 'gender performativity', 'parody' and 'drag', concepts and practices with which Butler has come to be widely associated, albeit somewhat misleadingly. Judith Butler (1956–) is Maxine Elliot Professor in Rhetoric and Comparative Literature at the University of California, Berkeley, yet this official academic title is somewhat deceptive, as she does not write explicitly about either rhetoric or comparative literature. There is yet more scope for possible confusion: very few critics and academics would associate Butler with Hegelian philosophy in the first instance, yet it is impossible to overestimate the influence of the nineteenth-century German philosopher G.W.F. Hegel (1770–1831) on Butler's work. Butler studied philosophy in the 1980s and her first book examined the impact of Hegel's work on twentieth-century French philosophers. Subsequent books draw extensively from psychoanalytic, feminist and post-structuralist theories, and the chapters that follow will emphasize the importance of all these theoretical frameworks to her extensive formulations of identity.

The potential 'misfit' between Butler's academic title and the person it is supposed to describe not only exemplifies the difficulties critics

and commentators experience in pinning her down both conceptually
and in terms of where to locate her within a broad intellectual field,
but it also reveals the instability of the terms by which people's identities are constituted. In later chapters we shall see that this is an aspect
of 'subject formation' with which Butler's work is pre-eminently
concerned. Indeed, if we did have to 'pin Butler down' (an endeavour
which would work against the Butlerian grain, if there is one), her
theorizations of gendered and sexed identity would probably be
regarded as her most important interventions in the diverse array
of academic fields with which she is connected. You would find her
best-known book, *Gender Trouble* (1990) and its 'sequel', *Bodies That
Matter* (1993) on many gender studies reading lists, and these two texts
are also likely to be studied by people working in the areas of queer
theory, feminist theory and gay and lesbian theory. Butler's other books
also deal with issues which are relevant to a range of academic disciplines, including philosophy, politics, law, sociology, film studies and
literary studies.

Evidently Butler's work in general, and her individual works in
particular, defy easy categorization, and yet this is part of what constitutes their challenge. To a greater or lesser extent, all Butler's books
ask questions about the formation of identity and subjectivity, tracing
the processes by which we become subjects when we assume the
sexed/gendered/'raced' identities which are constructed for us (and
to a certain extent by us) within existing power structures. Butler is
engaged in an ongoing interrogation of 'the subject' in which she asks
through what processes subjects come into existence, by what means
they are constructed, and how those constructions work and fail.
Butler's 'subject' is not an individual, but a linguistic structure in
formation. 'Subjecthood' is not a given, and since the subject is always
involved in the endless process of becoming, it is possible to reassume
or repeat subjecthood in different ways. '[W]ho will be a subject here,
and what will count as a life[?]', Butler asks in a recent article (WIC:
20): whom do I oppress by constructing a coherent identity for myself
and 'doing' my identity? What happens if our identities 'fail', and
might such failures provide opportunities for subversive *re*constructions
of identity? Perhaps those reconstructions, as subversive as they may
seem, will end up cohering into identity formations which are just as
oppressive in their own way. How can we tell what is subversive and
what merely consolidates power? And what degree of choice do we

have about how we 'do' our identities? By asking these questions I am jumping ahead somewhat, but this will give you an idea of the issues that will be explored in detail in the following chapters.

DIALECTIC

As you will see when you read Butler's texts, asking questions is a mode which she favours, yet you will seldom find her providing answers. The piling of question upon question can seem bewildering at times, but it is not just a stylistic flaw, and the withholding of answers is neither ignorance nor obtuseness on Butler's part. It is because, like the 'subjects' she discusses, Butler's works themselves are part of a process or a becoming which has neither origin nor end; indeed, in which origin and end are rejected as oppressively, perhaps even violently, linear or 'teleological' (i.e. moving towards a specific end or a final outcome). If you were to attempt to 'plot' Butler's work on a graph, you would not find her ideas progressing in a straight line from A to M to Z; instead, the movement of her thought would resemble a Mobius strip, or a series of Mobius strips, exemplifying how her theories curve or circle around issues without attempting to resolve them.

Although I am going to deal with Butler's work in chronological order, as you read it will be important to bear in mind that this is not meant to imply that there is a clear or linear progression from book to book. The idea of *process* or *becoming* will be crucial to understanding Butler's theories, which draw on the Hegelian notion of dialectic. Dialectic will be discussed in Chapter 2, but here it will be useful to offer a brief summary or a working definition. Dialectic is the mode of philosophical enquiry most commonly associated with Hegel (although he was not the first to formulate it), in which a thesis is proposed which is subsequently negated by its antithesis and resolved in a synthesis. This synthesis or resolution is not, however, final, but provides the basis for the next thesis, which once again leads to antithesis and synthesis before the process starts all over again. Within Butler's dialectical model, knowledge proceeds through opposition and cancellation, never finally reaching an 'absolute' or final certainty, but only positing ideas that cannot be fixed as 'truths'. The sciences, which many people regard as having some sort of authority or claim to 'truth', follow this similar movement through experiment, disagreement and revision: a neuroscientist who makes a 'discovery' about the operation of neurons in the brain will be drawing from previous research, as well as working in the knowledge that subsequent generations of neuroscientists may refute her or his findings or use them as the basis for further research. Likewise, although many philosophers and thinkers may have claimed to have discovered 'the truth', other philosophers and thinkers have come along and advanced alternative truth claims, which are again subsequently refuted by others.

Butler is not a thinker who claims to resolve the problems and issues she raises in her analyses and, for her, dialectic is an open-ended process. In fact, she regards resolution as dangerously anti-democratic, since ideas and theories that present themselves as self-evident 'truths' are often vehicles for ideological assumptions that oppress certain groups of people in society, particularly those in the minority or on the margins. An obvious and relevant example for Butler would be right-wing notions of homosexuality as 'wrong', 'unnatural', 'aberrant', and as something to be prohibited and punished. Such attitudes may present themselves as truthful or self-evidently 'right' in some (religious, moral, ideological) sense, but part of Butler's project is to prise such terms open, to contextualize and analyze their claims to truth, thereby making them available to interpretation and contestation. By 'such terms' I mean identity categories including 'gay', 'straight', 'bisexual', 'transsexual', 'black' and 'white', as well as notions such as 'truth', 'right' and 'norm'. Butler's work enters into dialectical engagement with the categories by which the subject is described and constituted, investigating *why* the subject is currently configured as it is and suggesting that alternative modes of description may be made available within existing power structures.

Many readers may find it frustrating and annoying that Butler provides no answers to the questions she poses, and some critics have gleefully pointed out what seem to be anomalies and contradictions in her theories. And yet, in dialectical spirit, Butler is willing to go back on herself and revise her positions, admitting when she has been wrong or unclear and maximizing the gaps in her writing as starting points for future critical and theoretical directions for herself and others. In this sense, her work enters into dialectical debate with itself, resembling the journey of the Spirit as described by Hegel in *Phenomenology of Spirit* (1807). Hegel's important book describes the progress of the Spirit towards absolute knowledge, but for Butler the

Phenomenology does not end with closure or resolution but is characterized by an open-endedness and *ir*resolution which contain more promise than teleology. This insight might equally apply to Butler's own theories and her formulations of identity as endless process and becoming.

INFLUENCES

Butler's theoretical analyses of the subject and the processes of subject formation constitute major critical and theoretical interventions into more than one academic field, yet this is not something Butler effected single-handedly and neither is Hegel her only philosophical influence. Butler herself would be the first to acknowledge that theorists and philosophers do not write in isolation and that there is nothing 'original' or unique about what they write. This is not only because their work necessarily exists in a dialectical relationship to the ideas and theories that precede them, but also because all statements are repetitions of previous statements that take place on the same signifying chain. This is an important idea to which we will return in later chapters (and it is certainly not 'original' to Butler); for now, I will sketch Butler's complex theoretical, philosophical and political affiliations.

I have already mentioned Hegel as a major influence on Butler, and her first book, *Subjects of Desire* (1987), analyzes the reception of Hegel's *Phenomenology of Spirit* by two generations of twentieth-century French philosophers. This might seem to be a very specific, not to mention arcane, subject, and yet two of the philosophers whose work Butler touches on in *Subjects* prove to be important influences on her future thought. The French philosopher Michel Foucault (1926–84) and his historical analyses of the variable constructions of sex and sexuality in different societies and contexts provide Butler with a theoretical framework for her own formulations of gender, sex and sexuality as unfixed and constructed entities, while the linguistic theories of another twentieth-century French thinker, Jacques Derrida (1930–), complement these formulations of the subject. If Butler and Foucault describe subject-formation as a process which must be placed within specific historical and discursive contexts in order to be understood, then Derrida similarly describes meaning as an 'event' that takes place on a citational chain with no origin or end, a theory that effectively deprives individual speakers of control over their utterances. Again, this post-structuralist theory of language is a key idea to which we will return in the chapters that follow, but you may find it is useful to refer to other books in the *Routledge Critical Thinkers* series that deal with post-structuralist thinkers such as Paul de Man (1919–83).

The importance of Foucault and Derrida to Butler's work has led many people to classify her as a post-structuralist, since this is the 'school of thought' (although it isn't one exactly) to which they are generally regarded as belonging. However, while she is undoubtedly influenced by post-structuralist modes of thinking and analysis, there are other equally important influences on Butler's work – in particular, psychoanalytic theory, feminist theory and Marxist theory – and some of these texts are listed along with their corresponding 'Butlerian' theories in the box below. Don't worry at this stage if ideas such as 'performativity' and 'citationality' are unfamiliar to you, since they will be analyzed in the chapters that follow.

Much of Butler's work reads psychoanalytic theory through a Foucauldian lens and Foucault through a psychoanalytic lens (this is particularly true of *The Psychic Life of Power*, 1997), in particular the work of Sigmund Freud (1856–1939) and the French post-structuralist psychoanalyst Jacques Lacan (1901–81), whose theories of sex, sexuality and gender have been of crucial importance to a number of feminist thinkers. Butler's work is heavily inflected by the writings of feminist thinkers, including the existentialist feminist philosopher Simone de Beauvoir (1908–86), Monique Wittig (1935–), Luce Irigaray (1932–) and the American anthropologist Gayle Rubin. As you read Butler's writings you will find her repeatedly returning to an important essay by the French post-structuralist Marxist thinker Louis Althusser (1918–90), in which he describes the structure and workings of ideology and what he calls 'ideological state apparatuses'.

Butler often approaches (and sometimes appropriates) the thinkers on whom her own ideas, to some extent, depend in a spirit of *critique* (as opposed to 'criticism'), a subject on which she has also written recently in her lecture 'What Is Critique?' (2000). Butler is neither a Freudian nor a Foucauldian, nor is she a Marxist, a feminist or a post-structuralist; instead, we might say that she shares affinities with these theories and their political projects, identifying with none of them in a singular sense but deploying a range of theoretical paradigms wherever it seems most appropriate in various, sometimes unexpected, combinations.

BUTLER'S INFLUENCES AND IDEAS

'WOMAN' AS A TERM-IN-PROCESS

Simone de Beauvoir: *The Second Sex* (1949)
Monique Wittig: 'The Straight Mind' (1980)
Gayle Rubin: 'The Traffic in Women: Notes on the "Political Economy" of Sex' (1975)

LORDSHIP AND BONDAGE/SLAVE MORALITY

G.W.F. Hegel: *Phenomenology of Spirit* (1807)
Friedrich Nietzsche: *On the Genealogy of Morals* (1887)

GENEALOGY/SUBJECTIVATION

Michel Foucault: *The History of Sexuality Vol. I* (1976); *Discipline and Punish: The Birth of the Prison* (1975)

MELANCHOLIA

Sigmund Freud: 'Mourning and Melancholia' (1917); *The Ego and the Id* (1923); *Civilisation and Its Discontents* (1930)

INTERPELLATION

Louis Althusser: 'Ideology and Ideological State Apparatuses' (1969)

THE LESBIAN PHALLUS

Jacques Lacan: 'The Signification of the Phallus' (1958)

PERFORMATIVITY AND CITATIONALITY

Jacques Derrida: 'Signature Event Context' (1972)
J.L. Austin: *How To Do Things With Words* (1955)

TEXTUALLY QUEER

It is because so much of Butler's work has been concerned with the ongoing analysis and resulting destabilization of the category of 'the subject' (a process she calls 'a critical genealogy of gender ontologies'), that she is regarded by many as *the* queer theorist par excellence. We have seen that, up until the late 1980s, Butler was working on Hegel and his reception by French philosophers, and the resulting book *Subjects of Desire* shows curiously little interest in the issues which were subsequently to preoccupy Butler, namely, the formation of the subject within sexed and gendered power structures. However, three early articles published at around this time, give a clear indication of Butler's future theoretical directions: 'Sex and Gender in Simone de Beauvoir's *Second Sex*' (1986) and 'Variations on Sex and Gender: Beauvoir, Wittig and Foucault' (1987) in many ways pave the way for *Gender Trouble*, published only a few years later, while 'Foucault and the Paradox of Bodily Inscriptions' (1989) considers the discursive construction of the body in Foucault's *The History of Sexuality Vol. I* and his *Discipline and Punish*. This is an issue to which Butler will return in *Bodies That Matter*, where she gives a much more extended analysis of the 'matter of sex' (see Chapter 3, this volume).

These articles give a clear indication of the key thinkers and theories from whom Butler draws, and the blend of Foucauldianism, psycho-analysis and feminism that characterizes her work from the start is part of what constitutes the 'queerness' of her theories. Indeed, in the 1980s, when Butler first entered the philosophical theoretical field, feminist theory began to interrogate (as Butler does) the category of 'the female subject' as a stable and self-evident entity. Under the influ-ence of Foucault, a number of theorists rejected the idea that 'sex' was the biologically determined entity it was previously taken to be, and instead they deployed Foucault's historical formulations of the ways in which sex and sexuality are discursively constructed over time and from culture to culture (although Foucault has been accused of neglecting culture). 'Woman' was no longer a category whose stability could be assumed as it often was in the liberatory feminist discourses of the 1960s and 1970s, as the categories of gender, sex and sexuality now came under the scrutiny of theorists such as Butler, Rubin and Eve Sedgwick (1950–).

Queer theory thus arose from a coalition (at times an uneasy one) of feminist, post-structuralist and psychoanalytic theories, which fa-cilitated and informed the ongoing investigation into the category of the subject. 'Queer' is a radical appropriation of a term which had previously been used to wound and abuse, and at least part of its radi-calism lies in its resistance to straightforward (so to speak) definition. Sedgwick, a queer theorist whose influential *Epistemology of the Closet* was published in 1990, the same year as *Gender Trouble*, characterizes queer as indistinguishable, undefinable, mobile. 'Queer is a continuing moment, movement, motive – recurrent, eddying, *troublant*' she writes in *Tendencies*, her collection of essays, pointing out that the Latin root of the words means *across*, coming from the Indo-Latin root *torquere* meaning 'to twist', and the English 'athwart' (Sedgwick 1994: xii). Queer thus exemplifies what the cultural theorist Paul Gilroy in his book *The Black Atlantic* (1993) identifies as a theoretical emphasis on routes rather than roots; in other words, queer is not concerned with definition, fixity or stasis, but is transitive, multiple and anti-assimilationist.

While gender studies, gay and lesbian studies and feminist theory may have assumed the existence of 'the subject' (i.e. the gay subject, the lesbian subject, the 'female', 'feminine' subject), queer theory undertakes an investigation and a deconstruction of these categories, affirming the indeterminacy and instability of all sexed and gendered identities. It is important to bear in mind that one of the defining contexts for queer theory in the 1980s and 1990s was the Aids virus and the anti-gay reactions of many upholders of 'straight culture' in response to what was (and still is) widely regarded as a 'gay plague'. In the face of such violent reactions, it is all the more important to investigate formulations of straightness in order to reveal the 'queerness' underlying particularly those identities which aggressively present themselves as straight, straightforward, singular and stable. Queer theorists, on the other hand, affirm the instability and indeterminacy of *all* gendered and sexed identities: while Sedgwick formulated the notion of 'homosexual panic' to describe straight culture's paranoid response to the multiple, shifting and indeterminate nature of sexual identities, Butler draws from Freud in her theorizations of heterosexuality as a 'melancholy' structure of identity which is based upon a socially imposed primary 'loss' or rejection of homosexual desire. Melancholic heterosexuality is one of Butler's most important contributions to queer theory, and it exemplifies the ethos of queer itself as a 'movement' (as Sedgwick characterizes it) that causes gender trouble. Indeed, it is in *Gender Trouble* that we will encounter Butler's formulations of melancholy gender and sexual identity.

PERFORMATIVITY

Performativity will be discussed in detail in Chapter 3 of this book, but at this stage it might be helpful to give you just a foretaste of this key Butlerian idea. We have already seen that Butler is less interested in 'the individual' and 'individual experience' (if there is any such thing), than in analyzing the processes by which the individual comes to assume her or his position as a subject. Rather than assuming that identities are self-evident and fixed as essentialists do, Butler's work traces the processes by which identity is constructed within language and discourse: constructivist theories do not attempt to reduce everything to linguistic constructions, but are interested in tracing the conditions of emergence of, in this case, the subject. The term Butler, following Foucault, uses to describe this mode of analysis is genealogical. Very briefly, genealogy is a mode of historical investigation that does not have 'the truth' or even knowledge as its goal. As Butler puts it, ' "Genealogy" is not the history of events, but the enquiry into the conditions of emergence (*Entstehung*) of what is called history, a moment of emergence that is not finally distinguishable from fabrication' (RBP: 15).

A genealogical investigation into the constitution of the subject will assume that sex and gender are the *effects* rather than the causes of institutions, discourses and practices; in other words, you as a subject do not create or cause institutions, discourses and practices, but they create or cause you by determining your sex, sexuality and gender. Butler's genealogical analyses will focus on how the subject-effect, as she calls it, comes about, and she will also suggest that there are ways in which the subject might be 'effected' differently. If the subject is not just 'there' from the beginning (i.e. from the moment it is born), but *instituted* in specific contexts and at specific times (so that birth itself is a scene of subjectivation, an example Butler uses), then the subject may be instituted differently in ways that do not simply reinforce existing power structures.

As we shall see in the chapters that follow, Butler's genealogical critique of the category of the subject dovetails with her notion that gendered and sexed identities are performative. Here Butler is extending de Beauvoir's famous insight that '[o]ne is not born, but rather becomes, a woman' (1949: 281) to suggest that 'woman' is something we 'do' rather than something we 'are'. Crucially, Butler is *not* suggesting that gender identity is a performance, since that would presuppose the existence of a subject or an actor who is *doing* that performance. Butler refutes this notion by claiming that the performance pre-exists the performer, and this counter-intuitive, apparently impossible argument has led many readers to confuse performativity with performance. She herself admits that, when she first formulated the idea, she did not differentiate clearly enough between performativity – a concept which we shall see has specific linguistic and philosophical underpinnings – and straightforward theatre. It is important to bear in mind that, like so many of Butler's formulations and like the identity categories she is describing, performativity is a shifting concept that gradually evolves over the course of several books. This makes it difficult to define with any certainty, but once again means that the form and method of Butler's writing enact the theory that it describes.

THE DEATH OF THE SUBJECT?

These ideas will be dealt with more fully in the chapters that follow where they will be discussed in the context of other, equally important (and often equally complex) theories. For many people the name 'Judith Butler' still means performative gender (or 'gender as performance' if they are simplifying) or parody and drag, even though this by no means does justice to the range and extent of her theories. Indeed, Butler's ideas have had a significant impact amongst feminist theorists, gay and lesbian theorists and queer theorists, and her work has been influential in a wide array of fields. (See 'After Butler' for a more extensive discussion of her influence.)

All the same, a number of Butler's critics have expressed their impatience with what they view as her over-attention to language and her concomitant neglect of the material and the political, and they accuse her of quietism (i.e. passivity), nihilism, and 'killing off' the subject; one recent philosopher has even claimed that Butler 'collaborates with evil', an extreme accusation that demonstrates, if nothing else, the violent reactions Butler's theories are likely to generate. On the other hand, many readers have found potential for political subversion in theories that consistently affirm the value of destabilizing and deconstructing the terms by which subjects and identities are constituted. The idea that the subject is not a pre-existing, essential entity and that our identities are constructed, means that it is possible for identities to be reconstructed in ways that challenge and subvert existing power structures. These are the issues and questions to which Butler repeatedly returns: What is power? What is subversion? How is it possible to tell the difference between the two?

THE POLITICS OF STYLE

Butler has expressed surprise at the critical debates generated by what she calls 'the popularisation of *Gender Trouble*', which, although 'interesting . . . ended up being a terrible misrepresentation of what I wanted to say!' (GP: 33). It is hardly surprising that Butler has, by her own admission, been misinterpreted and misunderstood, since the concepts with which she deals are philosophically challenging, often apparently 'counter-intuitive', and not always described in immediately accessible language. In 1999 the academic journal *Philosophy and Literature* voted Butler their number one 'bad writer' in an annual contest for 'the most stylistically lamentable passages found in scholarly books and articles', and in recent years it has often seemed that Butler's prose style is as likely to earn her critical attention as her ideas. It may be the case that complaining about Butler's prose style is a substitute for understanding her ideas, and an easy pretext for rejecting them, but you would not be alone if, like many readers, you found her writing infuriating; it may seem repetitive, interrogative, allusive and opaque, leaving you asking yourself after a few pages, why read Butler at all?

Butler's texts are certainly linguistically as well as conceptually demanding, but you should not be unduly troubled or altogether put off by their apparent obscurity and allusiveness, even if you find yourself lost or bewildered at times. Indeed, rather than simply dismissing Butler as a clumsy prose stylist or an arrogant thinker who does not bother to explain her concepts, it is important to recognize that Butler's style is *itself* part of the theoretical and philosophical interventions she is attempting to make (see 'After Butler'). As a thinker who is interested in language and acutely aware of the significance of linguistic discourse, it is highly unlikely that Butler has not thought about how to do things with words, and since she has frequently addressed the criticisms which have been levelled at her on this score, we may infer that this is indeed a pressing issue for her. In the Preface to the 1999 anniversary edition of *Gender Trouble* Butler acknowledges that, for some readers, it must be 'strange, and maddening' to be confronted by a text that does not go out of its way to be easily consumed, but may in fact do precisely the opposite. However, Butler refutes the 'common-sense' view that a 'good' prose style is necessarily a lucid one, affirming that neither style nor grammar is politically neutral. It would be inconsistent for Butler to contest gender norms, which she claims are linguistically constructed and mediated, without also contesting the very language and grammar in which those norms are instituted. Furthermore, we will see that part of her ongoing project is to cause 'trouble' by drawing attention to the instabilities and incoherencies of sex and gender and the political potential of these. Again, the language Butler deploys is part of this political strategy, and it is clear that her prose style is strategically and *deliberately* challenging rather than the symptom of a muddled mind.

In *Subjects of Desire*, Butler describes the prose style of Hegel, another notoriously 'difficult' philosopher, and it is intriguing to read the following comments on his *Phenomenology of Spirit* in the light of her own ideas about language and prose style:

> Hegel's sentences *enact* the meanings that they convey; indeed, they show that what 'is' only is to the extent that is *enacted*. Hegelian sentences are read with difficulty, for their meaning is not immediately given or known; they call to be reread, read with different intonations and grammatical emphases. Like a line of poetry that stops us and forces us to consider that the *way* in which it is said is essential to *what* it is saying, Hegel's sentences rhetorically draw attention to themselves. The discrete and static words on the page deceive us only momentarily into thinking that discrete and static meanings will be released by our reading. If we refuse to give up the expectation that univocal meanings linearly arranged will unfold from the words at hand, we will find Hegel confused, unwieldy, unnecessarily dense. But if we question the presumptions of the Understanding that the prose asks us to, we will experience the incessant movement of the sentence that constitutes its meaning.
>
> (SD: 18–19)

'Confused, unwieldy, and unnecessarily dense' is exactly how frustrated readers might describe Butler's prose, but here she suggests that this apparent obscurity and difficulty is part of the point (in fact, it is inseparable from the point). By reading Hegel's (and Butler's) prose carefully and painstakingly, the reader will actually *experience* what the philosophers are describing, appropriately enough, 'the Understanding' in the instance Butler cites: the prose enacts what it describes, an idea that is similar to Butler's formulations of linguistic performativity and recitation. Moreover, like 'queer' itself, that movement or mood with which Butler's writings are most frequently identified, Butler's sentences are 'troubling' in their openness to interpretation, their refusal to be pinned down to a single meaning, and their creative vulnerability to 'misinterpretation' and error. It is in this sense that her prose enacts the deconstruction that it names, and in later chapters we shall look more closely at the ways in which this 'theory-in-style' operates.

AGAINST DEFINITION

If Butler's prose style is not merely a vehicle for politics but effectively *enacts* the politics that it describes, then clearly my account of Butler's theories will be no substitute for reading the books themselves. Although I do not intend to emulate Butler's inimitable and demanding prose style, the necessarily limited summary of her work that follows is written in a similar spirit of open-endedness and lack of resolution or closure. I am not attempting to define Butler's theories, and the reader should approach what *do* look like definitions with caution, since they are not meant to be authoritative or final. Perhaps these warnings will seem unnecessary, since not even Butler would claim to have the final word on Butler, but I think it is important to draw attention to the element of appropriation, perhaps even 'violence' of a certain kind, that takes place in any interpretation of any thinker or writer, particularly when that thinker conveys her ideas in a way which in itself constitutes a political challenge.

The chapters that follow will look at Butler's work in chronological order, focusing on what might be identified as five major areas of her thought: *the subject*; *gender*; *sex*; *language*; and *the psyche*. It would be neat and convenient to plot a 'progression' from one issue to another, but we have already seen that Butler's work defies this sort of linear patterning and you will find that each of these topics is dealt with to a greater or lesser degree in each of her texts. I have already characterized Butler's writing as entering into a dialectical relationship with itself, and this means that issues that are raised and debated in one text are picked up, reanalyzed, and revised in the next. Indeed, Butler is not an author who is afraid to repeat herself and, fully aware of the subversive potential of repetition, at times she ironically cites and re-cites her own arguments inter- and intratextually. Again, this has the effect of preventing closure and preserving an interpretive democratic open-endedness, although as you read the chapters that follow and Butler's texts themselves you may well find yourself wondering about the political efficacy of what appears to be a pre-eminently *textual* strategy. If you do experience difficulties or doubts as you go along, it may be useful to bear in mind the model Butler suggests for a 'successful' reading of Hegel: as readers we should relinquish our expectations of linear, 'univocal' (i.e. singular) meanings, questioning our own presumptions in order to 'experience the incessant movement of the sentence that constitutes its meaning' (SD: 19).

KEY IDEAS

THE SUBJECT

CONTEXT

Butler's analysis of 'the subject' begins in her first book, *Subjects of Desire*, a text that has assumed a variety of different forms. Originally submitted as a dissertation at Yale University in 1984, the work was revised in 1985–6, published in 1987, and not reprinted until 1999. In the Preface to the 1999 edition Butler calls *Subjects of Desire* a piece of juvenilia which was published too early, and she asks for her reader's 'abundant forgiveness in reserve' for a work which, she claims, would now require extensive rewriting and revision (SDII: viii). The subject of *Subjects* might indeed seem anomalous to the reader for whom 'Judith Butler' signifies formulations of queer identity and discussions of gender and the body, neither of which seem to be much in evidence in this study of Hegel and twentieth-century French philosophy. In spite of this, and notwithstanding the author's retrospective disclaimers, it is an important philosophical text in its own right, and it also contains a number of the ideas Butler develops in later, better-known works.

Subjects originally dealt with the reception of Hegel's *Phenomenology of Spirit* by French philosophers of the 1930s and 1940s. In her Preface to the 1999 paperback edition of the book Butler explains that, as a Fulbright scholar at Heidelberg University in Germany, she trained mainly in continental philosophy, studying key thinkers such as Karl Marx (1818–83) and Hegel, along with Martin Heidegger (1889–1976), Søren Kierkegaard (1813–55), Maurice Merleau-Ponty (1908–61) and critical theorists of the Frankfurt school. In the 1970s and 1980s Butler had only dabbled in the post-structuralist theories of Derrida and de Man, and she writes that it was later, at a Women's Studies Faculty seminar, that she 'discovered' Foucault, whose writings were to influence her own to a great extent. After leaving Yale to take up a position as a postdoctoral Fellow at Wesleyan University in the States, Butler became receptive to the French theory she had previously resisted, and when she revised her dissertation she added sections on the next generation of French philosophers – Lacan, Foucault and Gilles Deleuze (1925–95) – which had not been part of the original study.

Butler acknowledges the continuity between her early and late work in the 1999 Preface, where she claims that her interest in Hegelian formulations of the subject, desire and recognition runs throughout her writing: 'In a sense, all my work remains within the orbit of a certain set of Hegelian questions: What is the relation between desire and recognition, and how is it that the constitution of the subject entails a radical and constitutive relation to alterity?' (SDII: xiv). Butler 'returns' to Hegel in *The Psychic Life of Power*, and she has published articles on Hegel, feminism and phenomenology (see Further Reading). Perhaps most importantly, *Subjects* asks whether subjectivity necessarily rests upon the negation of the 'Other' by the 'Self', an idea to which Butler repeatedly returns.

KEY STRANDS OF CRITICAL THOUGHT

PHENOMENOLOGY

This is the study of consciousness, or the way in which things appear to us. The term has been used since the eighteenth century and is associated with the philosophy of Immanuel Kant (1724–1804) and G.W.F. Hegel (1770–1831) in the nineteenth century, and Edmund Husserl (1859–1938), Martin Heidegger (1889–1976), Jean-Paul Sartre (1905–80) and Maurice Merleau-Ponty (1908–61) in the twentieth century.

There are many different strands to phenomenology, so it is not easy to summarize in a sentence or two, but, for Husserl, the world as experienced in consciousness is the starting point for phenomenology. Very broadly speaking, it is concerned with how the mind perceives what is external to it, i.e. the perception of the essence of things.

FRANKFURT SCHOOL

This comprises philosophers, cultural critics and social scientists associated with the Institute for Social Research founded in Frankfurt in 1929. Key thinkers include Max Horkheimer (1895–1973), Theodor Adorno (1903–69), Herbert Marcuse (1898–1979), Erich Fromm (1900–80), Walter Benjamin (1892–1940) and Jürgen Habermas (1929–). The Frankfurt School is usually divided into three phases and two generations, moving through historical materialism, critical theory and 'the critique of instrumental reason'. Habermas, who belongs to the second generation, emphasizes the importance of normative foundations and interdisciplinary research.

STRUCTURALISM

This is a movement that largely took place in France, stemming from the work of the linguist Ferdinand de Saussure (1857–1913). Key thinkers include the anthropologist Claude Lévi-Strauss (1908–) and the cultural and literary critic Roland Barthes (1915–80). Structuralism, as its name suggests, focuses on the analysis of structures and systems rather than content.

POST-STRUCTURALISM

This is a much-disputed term that is sometimes used interchangeably with *deconstruction*. Key thinkers associated with post-structuralism include Jacques Derrida (1930–), Paul de Man (1919–83) and Michel Foucault (1926–84). Deconstructive critique sets out to undermine Western metaphysics by contesting and undoing *binary oppositions*, revealing their idealism and their reliance on an *essential centre* or *presence*. A deconstructive reading of a text never arrives at a final or complete meaning, since meaning is never self-present but is a process continually taking place. The author is no longer taken to be the source of meaning for a text, and Roland Barthes accordingly announced 'the death of the author' in his essay of that title.

HEGEL'S UNHAPPY HERO

The German title of *Phenomenology of Spirit* is *Phänomenologie des Geistes*, where '*Geist*' may be very loosely translated either as 'spirit' or 'mind', and in it Hegel charts the progress of an increasingly self-conscious Spirit towards absolute knowledge. Hegel's '*Geist*' resembles the protagonist of fictional narratives in which the hero (and it is usually a male) gradually progresses from ignorance to enlightenment and self-knowledge, and although the Spirit is not exactly the same as Butler's 'subject', it is sufficiently close that the two terms will nevertheless be used more or less interchangeably in this chapter. Contemporary philosopher Jonathan Rée compares Hegel's account of the Spirit's metaphysical 'journey' to texts such as Homer's *Odyssey* (*c*.750–700 BC), Dante's *Divine Comedy* (*c*.1307–21) and Bunyan's *Pilgrim's Progress* (1678–84), in each of which the hero's experiences on his travels lead him towards the state of greater wisdom, or Christian enlightenment, which he ultimately attains. Rée writes that Hegel's *Phenomenology* is a story, 'the story of Spirit – or Everyman – "the universal individual" – travelling the long road leading from the dull realm of "natural" consciousness to absolute knowledge and "working its passage" through every possible philosophical system on its way' (1987: 76–7).

Although *Phenomenology* is the story of the Spirit's progress towards absolute knowledge, unlike the narratives I have just mentioned Hegel's Spirit does not actually go anywhere, since its 'journey' is a metaphysical one that also stands for the progress of world history. 'Phenomenology' may be described very generally as the study of the way things appear to us and the nature of perception, so that Hegel's *Phenomenology* is a study of successive forms of consciousness. 'Absolute Knowledge' is knowledge of the world as it really is, and at the end of *Phenomenology* we discover that this ultimate reality resides in our own minds. In other words, everything in the material world is a construct of consciousness, which is why it is so important to understand how consciousness functions, or how it is that we come to know. Absolute knowledge is only reached when the mind grasps the fact that reality is not independent of it, and that what it is striving to know is really *itself*.

The *Phenomenology* is also frequently compared to a *Bildungsroman* or novel of experience. Literally translated from the German, *Bildungsroman* means 'formation' or 'education novel', i.e. a novel which documents the formation or education of its protagonist. Examples of this genre might include Frances Burney's *Evelina, or a Young Lady's Entrance Into the World* (1778), J.W. Goethe's *Wilhelm Meister* (1795), Charles Dickens' *Great Expectations* (1860–1), and James Joyce's *Portrait of the Artist as a Young Man* (1914–15); it would seem that the *Bildungsroman* is usually by men and about men. These novels chart the metaphorical or literal journey of the hero or heroine from inexperience and ignorance to experience, and, like Bunyan's Christian or Burney's Evelina, the Spirit commits a series of errors during the course of its educational journey, acknowledging each mistake as it goes along and assimilating the lesson afforded by the error before moving on to the next stage.

This progression from error to enlightenment to increased self-knowledge is a movement that may be characterized as *dialectical*, a key term in the Hegelian lexicon (see 'Why Butler?'). Dialectic is not a philosophical method (although it is sometimes regarded as such), but a movement from one apparently secure position (thesis) to its opposite (antithesis), before a reconciliation of the two is brought about (synthesis). In an article on the twentieth-century American poet, Wallace Stevens, Butler cites Hegel's definition of dialectic as 'the unity of apparent opposites – more precisely . . . the logical and ontological relation of mutual implication that persists between ostensibly oppositional terms' (NTI: 269). In other words, to make any affirmation (e.g. 'God exists'; 'Australia is a big country') is to presuppose that such a statement or thesis could be denied by its antithesis, so that, as Hegel asserts, there is a relation of 'mutual implication' between terms which appear to be opposites.

In the context of *Phenomenology* or a *Bildungsroman*, a dialectical movement would be the progression from belief through error to recognition and experience, ultimately resulting in absolute knowledge. Not all syntheses are as final as that however, and it is likely that the synthesis will form the next link in the dialectical chain: the synthesis is the starting point for the next thesis and the antithesis and synthesis following on from it. The Spirit progresses by acknowledging the mistakes it has made, so that its life journey resembles a game of snakes and ladders in which it repeatedly moves upwards or forwards, only to slither back down again when it commits an error before moving on to the next stage. (Jonathan Rée also compares the *Phenomenology* to 'a kind of map or game' (1987: 84)). Hegel's subject is therefore a subject-in-progress, that, as Rée points out, can only build itself by ceaselessly destroying itself (or falling down the ladder), fleeing in horror from its previous errors and finding itself in its utter dismemberment (1987: 81). The Spirit progresses by negating everything that falls in its way without ever being certain that a happy ending ultimately awaits it, and it is only once it has passed through the successive stages that Hegel describes – sense-certainty, perception, force and understanding, self-certainty, stoicism, scepticism, unhappy consciousness, reason, logic, psychology, reason, and so on – that it finally reaches its ultimate destination of absolute knowledge.

DESTINATION DESIRE

Butler describes Hegel's journeying Spirit (which she claims is always a 'he' (SD: 20)) as a comic figure, a cartoon character who is never put off by the reversals and obstacles it encounters in its way. 'What seems like tragic blindness turns out to be more like the comic myopia of Mr Magoo whose automobile careening through the neighbor's chicken coop always seems to land on all four wheels', she writes. 'Like such miraculously resilient characters of the Sunday morning cartoon, Hegel's protagonists always reassemble themselves, prepare a new scene, enter the stage armed with a new set of ontological insights – and fail again' (SD: 21). Hegel's *Geist* is thus a hopeful subject, 'a fiction of infinite capability, a romantic traveler who only learns from what he experiences' (SD: 22), and yet at the same time he is a deluded and impossible figure who, like Don Quixote, tilts at ontological windmills in his pursuit of reality (SD: 23).

HEGEL: SOME KEY TERMS

GEIST

Hegel's 'spirit' or 'mind', *Geist* is difficult to translate and just as difficult to define as a philosophical category. In his *Hegel Dictionary*, Michael Inwood gives nine interrelated definitions of *Geist*; these include: the human mind and its products; 'the subjective Spirit'; the intellect; Absolute Spirit (i.e. the infinite, self-consciousness of God); *Weltgeist* (world Spirit); *Volksgeist* (Spirit of the people) and *Geist der Zeit* (the Spirit of an age).

AUFHEBUNG

Literally translated, this means 'sublation'; again, any definition of this word will inevitably be reductive and simplistic, since the German verb *aufheben* contains three distinct meanings: 1) to raise, hold, lift up; 2) to annul, abolish, destroy, cancel; and 3) to keep, save or preserve. The last two meanings may appear to be contradictory, but these are the two to which Hegel explicitly refers. However, as Inwood points out, the first definition is still an aspect of *Aufhebung*, since the product of sublation is higher than the sum of its parts. *Aufhebung* therefore refers to the unifying or synthesizing of opposites into a form in which they are simultaneously cancelled and preserved. You could think of what happens to an individual brick, when, along with other bricks, cement, wood, glass, etc., it is used to build (for example) a library. The brick is still discernibly a brick, but it is now also a necessary part of a larger structure (the library), so that its 'identity' as an individual brick has been simultaneously cancelled and transcended (since it is now part of a building and not an individual brick) and preserved (since we can still see that it is a brick).

DIALECTIC

This is a mode of reasoning in which thesis leads to antithesis and is resolved in synthesis. Butler quotes the following from Hegel's *Logic*: 'Wherever there is movement, wherever there is life, wherever anything is carried into effect in the actual world, there Dialectic is at work' (NTI: 282).

ABSOLUTE KNOWLEDGE

This constitutes knowledge of what 'truly is'; the mind's realization that what it has been seeking to know is in fact itself.

ONTOLOGY

This is the science or study of being.

What motivates the Spirit in his travels, what prevents him from simply giving up at the successive stages of his journey when he discovers his own error, is *desire* – the desire to overcome the obstacles placed in his way, but, more crucially, the desire to know himself. Paraphrasing Hegel, Butler describes desire as the incessant effort to overcome external differences, which are finally revealed to be immanent features of the subject itself (SD: 6). Desire, in other words, is intimately connected to the process of coming into consciousness and the subject's increasing capacity for self-knowledge: it is 'an interrogative mode of being, a corporeal questioning of identity and place' (SD: 9), not merely denoting sexual desire or 'the kind of focused wanting that usually goes by that name' (SD: 99), but, specifically in this context, the desire for recognition and self-consciousness. Butler points out that the German word for desire, *Begierde,* signals animal desire as well as the philosophical desire that she claims Hegel is describing in the *Phenomenology*, where the subject eventually comes to know itself through the recognition and overcoming of difference (SD: 33).

In the Introduction to *Subjects* Butler sketches in the importance of desire for successive generations of philosophers, asking whether desire is rational and moral and whether it can be integrated into a philosophical project (SD: 3), or whether, on the other hand, it is philosophically dangerous, 'a principle of irrationality' (SD: 3). Only if desire is moral is a philosophical life feasible, and what follows in Butler's study is a consideration of how two generations of French philosophers adopt, adapt or challenge Hegel's specific formulations of desire and subjectivity. As you read on, bear in mind that, in this context, desire is defined as the impulse to know, and that, as we have seen, this is always a desire for self-consciousness.

SELF AND OTHER

Hegel writes that it is only through recognizing and knowing *another* that the 'Self' can know itself, so that desire is always desire for something 'Other', which turns out to be a desire for the subject *itself* (SD: 34). There are two modes of desiring in *Phenomenology*: the desire for the Other, leading to the loss of the Self, and the desire for ourselves (or, in other words, self-consciousness) which leads to the loss of the world (SD: 34). To put this another way, the subject can only know itself *through another*, but in the process of recognizing itself and constituting its own self-consciousness it must overcome or annihilate the Other, otherwise it places its own existence at risk (SD: 37). Desire, in other words, is tantamount to the *consumption* of the Other.

It would seem that self-consciousness is always a negative destructive process, and it is not the first time Butler has described the Spirit as metaphorically (and metaphysically) *hungry*: in the Introduction to

Subjects of Desire, she invokes a 'self-sufficient yet metaphysically secure Hegelian subject, that omnivorous adventurer of the Spirit who turns out, after a series of surprises, to *be* all that he encounters along his dialectical way' (SD: 6). Again, it is important to bear in mind that it isn't *animal* hunger or desire that motivates him, since here consumption is a means of encountering the Other and absorbing it into the Self. This process is described by the Hegelian term *Aufhebung* which translates roughly as *supersession* or *sublation* and means three things at once – to lift up, to cancel and to preserve – even though these alternative meanings might seem irreconcilable. Butler defines *Aufhebung* as a 'developing sequence' of desire, 'consuming desire, desire for recognition, desire for another's desire' (SD: 43). It is only through the supersession or sublation of another that the Spirit can recognize itself, a relationship of subjugation and overcoming that is outlined by Hegel in the 'Lordship and Bondage' section of *Phenomenology* where he formulates the philosophically influential *master/slave dialectic*.

LORDSHIP AND BONDAGE

In this important section of *Phenomenology* Hegel claims that self-consciousness can only know itself through another, but this process of self-recognition in another is not straightforward, for the Other that the Self has to overcome is in fact a part of itself (1807: 111). At this stage of its development, self-consciousness is split, lost, alienated in a kind of negative narcissism that is characterized by (self-)violence and hatred. The crucial point to grasp here is that this is not a literal confrontation, but one that takes place between two self-opposed parts of a consciousness that is split. Hegel characterizes these two 'halves' of consciousness as 'unequal and opposed . . . one is the independent consciousness whose essential nature is to be for itself, the other is the dependent consciousness whose essential nature is simply to live or to be for another. The former is lord, the other is bondsman' (1807: 115). Hegel paradoxically asserts that the lord is a self-contained consciousness which requires another consciousness in order to sustain its own independence, i.e. the lord needs the bondsman, to confirm his own sense of Self. The bondsman on the other hand, is busy working away, achieving through his labour 'pure being-for-self' (1807: 117). Far from being alienated by his labour, the worker recognizes the independence of his own consciousness through the creation of an object, whereas, in order to know himself, the lord must destroy both the bondsman and the thing on which he labours, and again, desire is the motivating force here (1807: 109).

Butler describes the confrontation between master and slave as a struggle to the death, for '[o]nly through the death of the Other will the initial self-consciousness retrieve its claim to autonomy' (SD: 49). The Otherness that the self-consciousness seeks to overcome is actually its *own* Otherness which it confronts in the bondsman, so that self-consciousness must repeatedly destroy itself in order to know itself. Self and Other are not only intimately related to each other; in fact, they *are* each other, and it is through their mutual recognition that they bring each other into being. If, as Butler claims, Self and Other are mutually-authoring, then desire is not a purely consumptive activity as it was previously characterized, but an ambiguous exchange in which two self-consciousnesses affirm their simultaneous autonomy and alienation from each other (SD: 50–1).

Butler describes this struggle to the life and death as an erotic encounter in which self-confronting subjects attempt to overcome their bodily limits, again, in order to know the Other and thereby the Self. At this point, the lord's desire is the desire to live, since death would signal the end of desire, and the bondsman also expresses a desire to live through his labour. However, unlike the lord he finds that he can transform the external world into a reflection of himself, thus gaining independence and freedom. As the lord becomes schooled in knowledge, the bondsman simultaneously acquires freedom, resulting in a gradual reversal of the roles the two subjects initially assumed.

There are now, it seems, two strands to desire: the desire for recognition by another self-consciousness so that it can recognize itself; and the desire to transform the natural world in order to gain autonomy and self-recognition. We gain recognition both through our bodies (the forms we inhabit in the world) and our work (the forms we create *of* the world), so that evidently there is an important connection between subjectivity, labour and community. Indeed, it is only by being in and of a community that the subject can acquire the identity for which it is searching, since as Butler puts it, '[t]rue subjectivities come to flourish only in communities that provide for reciprocal recognition, for we do not come to ourselves through work alone, but through the acknowledging look of the Other who confirms us' (SD: 58).

This is a crucial point, and one to which we will return when we look at French philosophers' interpretations and conceptualizations of Hegel's *Phenomenology*. The Spirit or *Geist* is a *collective* entity, one that cannot come into being or exist in isolation of its society, and the Spirit desires others in order to establish its intersubjectivity (SD: 58). This is the 'reformulation of desire as the articulation of historical identity and historical place' as Butler puts it. The rest of *Subjects of Desire* gives extensive analyses of twentieth-century French philosophers' readings and reconstitutions of the Hegelian subject, 'that struggling individual on the brink of collective identity' who requires the recognition of the Other he negates in order to know himself (SD: 58).

BROKEN SPIRITS

If *Phenomenology of Spirit* is a *Bildungsroman* featuring a subject-hero who embarks on a journey for absolute knowledge, *Subjects of Desire* could be described as a *Bildungsroman* in reverse, where the coherence of the apparently self-identical Hegelian subject is successively disintegrated in the works of two generations of twentieth-century French philosophers. This is certainly how Butler sees it, and her own philosophical 'narrative' describes how Hegel's intrepid and self-sufficient adventurer is shattered, its unity dispersed by the formulations of these philosophers. Butler's analysis of the French reception of Hegel starts with the philosopher Alexandre Kojève (1902–68), whose important *Introduction to the Reading of Hegel* was published in 1941. Butler goes on to analyze the 'Hegelian reflections' of Jean Hyppolite (1907–68), Jean-Paul Sartre (1905–80), Lacan, and the next generation of philosophers, Derrida, Deleuze and Foucault, concluding with a very brief section on Julia Kristeva (1941–).

Placing Kojève, Hyppolite and Sartre in the context of the renewed interest in Hegel in France during the 1930s and 1940s, Butler asks whether Hegel's self-identical 'metaphysically ensconced' subject was still a viable philosophical ideal at a historical juncture characterized by dislocation, metaphysical rupture and ontological isolation (i.e. there was a world war on at the time) (SD: 6). The Hegelian subject certainly proves to be a philosophical impossibility for the next generation of philosophers, Lacan, Deleuze and Foucault, for whom desire signals the disintegration of what is taken to be Hegel's coherent ontological entity. However, Butler argues that these thinkers misread Hegel's formulations of subjectivity while remaining within the terms of the Hegelian dialectical mode of analysis they are attempting to 'overcome'.

It is in this sense that *Subjects of Desire* is, as Butler describes it, a 'genealogy' of the metaphorical 'travels' of the Hegelian subject in twentieth-century France, and yet Butler emphasizes that Hegel's subject is not exactly as these philosophers describe it: 'the Hegelian subject is not a self-identical subject who travels smugly from one onto-logical place to another; it *is* its travels, and *is* every place in which it finds itself' she writes (SD: 8). The philosophical term for an identity which is constituted by whatever it comes into contact with is *the doctrine of internal relations*, and Butler claims that, while the doctrine of internal relations apparently provides the subject with autonomy, its lack of fixed boundaries means that, from the outset, it is less stable than it appears to be. The Hegelian subject is thus a subject-in-process whose instability and porousness deny it a fixed or final place in the world, a protagonist in what Butler calls a 'comedy of errors', a journey (or a drama) which we have seen involves repeated error, misrecog-nition and self-reconstitution.

BEYOND DIALECTIC

The twentieth-century French philosophers Butler analyzes in *Subjects of Desire* all attempt to move beyond and outside Hegelian dialectic as a philosophical mode. In *Subjects* Butler seems to take this for granted, but in an essay published a few years later she is more explicit as to why twentieth-century philosophers, particularly post-structuralist and postmodern thinkers who reject what Butler calls 'Hegel's romantic postulation of the dialectical unity of opposites', would wish to negate Hegel, although Butler also argues that dialectic without synthesis re-emerges in twentieth-century philosophical thought (NTI: 269). Although twentieth-century philosophers may still long for the kind of unity posited by Hegel, it is accompanied by their awareness that the notion of 'a dialectical unity of opposites' is now untenable, particularly in the context of post-structuralist formulations of language as an open field of possible meanings where emphasis is placed on difference rather than unity, and on interpretive openness rather than closure.

STRUCTURALISM AND POST-STRUCTURALISM

The structuralist linguist Ferdinand de Saussure (1857–1913) theorized language as a system of differences with no positive forms. There is no inherent connection between the *sign* (e.g. the word 'tree') and its *referent* (e.g. the living organisms you find growing in parks), but a sign only derives meaning from its position within the system of language as a whole. *Signifiers* (e.g. 'tree') are differentially connected to other signifiers, but again, they are not *necessarily* connected to their *signifieds* (i.e. the thing they are referring to). Language, in other words, is a *system of difference*. While departing from de Saussure in many respects, post-structuralist thinkers such as Jacques Derrida develop this insight: for Derrida, *différance* means at once difference and deferral, referring to the way in which signification is dependent on what is absent. Meaning is endlessly deferred, and it is in this sense that language is an open system of signs, while meaning can never be self-present or ultimately defined.

The question remains as to how twentieth-century French philosophers can reject or negate Hegel without enacting a philosophical move that is *itself* dialectical, and therefore implicitly Hegelian. Butler repeatedly makes the point that these thinkers deploy a dialectical mode of reasoning in the very act of refuting it, and she also argues that Hegel may be rescued from the accusation that he is a thinker who totalizes and unifies, so that phenomenology may provide some useful points of departure for feminist theory.

KOJÈVE, HYPPOLITE AND SARTRE

It is not a coincidence that the early twentieth-century French philosophers whose work Butler surveys in *Subjects of Desire* turned to Hegel during the 1930s and 1940s: prior to that, it seems that there was little interest in Hegel in France, but Butler claims that his appeal lay in the fact that his work fulfilled political and philosophical needs in this context and at this time (SD: 61). Butler quotes the claim of French phenomenologist Merleau-Ponty in 1946 that 'all the great philosophical ideas of the past century – the philosophies of Marx and Nietzsche, phenomenology, German existentialism and psychoanalysis – had their beginnings in Hegel' (SD: 61), and although she questions the 'exuberance' of asserting a single source for *all* subsequent philosophy, Butler nonetheless sees this as symptomatic of the intellectual climate of the time.

The second chapter of *Subjects*, 'Historical Desires: The French Reception of Hegel', begins with an analysis of desire and historical agency in Kojève's *Introduction to the Reading of Hegel*, before discussing Hyppolite's reading of Kojève reading Hegel and Sartre's existential reformulations of the Hegelian subject. These three philosophers are regarded as partly responsible for what has been called 'the triumph of Hegelianism in post-war France – a triumph forced by the vogue of existentialism' (Eribon 1991: 19), and it is important to note the connections between these thinkers and their philosophical contemporaries and successors.

Hyppolite was a contemporary of Sartre and Merleau-Ponty at the École normale supérieure in Paris; Kojève's lectures on Hegel were delivered between 1933 and 1939 and they were attended by Lacan and Merleau-Ponty, while Foucault was taught (briefly) by Hyppolite. To give an account of Butler's account of twentieth-century philosophers' accounts of Hegel might well seem convoluted, but the key point to bear in mind as you read is that these thinkers reject and revise Hegel's formulations of the subject, and that the way in which each thinker reconceptualizes the Hegelian subject may be regarded as symptomatic of the specific philosophical 'moment' at which she or he is writing.

EXISTENTIALISM

This is a philosophical movement particularly prominent in Europe after the Second World War. Existentialist thinkers include Jean-Paul Sartre (1905–80), Albert Camus (1913–60) and Simone de Beauvoir (1908–86). Martin Heidegger (1889–1976) and Maurice Merleau-Ponty (1908–61) are sometimes also described as existentialist philosophers. Like phenomenology, existentialism is not a movement or a philosophical school, and existentialist thinkers have put forward many different arguments.

Existentialists tend to focus on the uniqueness of individuals rather than analysing abstract human qualities. People cannot be defined by philosophical and psychological doctrines, since they are what they choose to be. This means that they must accept responsibility for their characters and their deeds rather than blaming external factors that are beyond their control. Sartre emphasizes that the individual is the source of all value, and he claims that individuals are obliged to make their own life-choices. To be conscious of such freedom is one of the conditions of 'authentic existence', whereas people who act in bad faith attempt to escape from anxiety, loneliness and terror by deceiving themselves that they are bound to act in certain ways. It is in these moments of anguish that the human condition reveals itself, and existentialists prioritize a moral life character-ized by sincerity and creativity.

In the lectures which comprise the *Introduction to the Reading of Hegel* Kojève reads Hegel's *Phenomenology* as an account of man's [*sic*] desires and the attempt to satisfy them. Kojève sees the master/slave dialectic as motivated by desire (the desire to be), a dialectical encounter which will culminate in the slave's emancipation through work. Kojève's reading of *Phenomenology* has been seen as an anthropocentric, existen-tial, 'atheistic' appropriation which is not 'true' to the spirit of Hegel's Spirit: this is because Kojève does not look forward to the resolution of dialectic in absolute knowledge, but anticipates instead 'the end of history', a view which is said to characterize 'postmodernist' thinkers with whom Kojève is often associated (e.g. Foucault, Deleuze and Derrida). Since Kojève emphasizes historicity rather than eternity, his own post-historical reading of Hegel underscores the temporality of *Phenomenology* by reading it through a Marxist–humanist lens in which the idea of *Geist* is replaced by that of 'man' (humanism) and God is seen as man's projection of himself (a strand of Marxist thought). At the end of history man recognizes that God is a creation, thereby over-coming his own alienation and at the same time confronting his own finitude. Living in the face of death without the props of external divine agency is what constitutes 'the end of history' and it is the only way to achieve existential freedom.

As Butler points out, this emphasis on temporality and historicity opens up *Phenomenology* to conflicting readings and new interpretations that reflect the historical contingency of reading itself (SD: ix). Butler's analysis of Kojève's *Introduction* focuses on the so-called 'heroism' of Kojève's subject of desire as he struggles to acquire consciousness through a dialectical encounter with the Other. Kojève's subject knows itself through its desire but desire can only be resolved through the negation of the Other, so that, as in *Phenomenology*, we find ourselves in the presence of two mutually conflicting subjectivities (master and slave) that are attempting to cancel each other out. As Kojève characterizes it the encounter is a historical one, and it is for this reason that desire can in fact *never* be resolved or overcome, since there is no real end to history. Butler argues that this frees Kojève from the teleological constraints of Hegel's *Phenomenology*, since in the *Introduction* dialectic is characterized as movement without end rather than a movement towards ultimate closure or 'telos'. The 'heroism' of Kojève's subject lies in the triumph of its individuality over collectivity, a form of individualism that Butler calls a 'brand of democratic Marxism', which would take place in an ideal Hegelian society where a dialectical mediation of individuality and collectivity has been achieved (SD: 78).

The next generation of philosophers acknowledge the importance of Kojève's theories for their own formulations of history, Hegel and the desiring subject. Kojève's 'heroic narrative of the human Spirit' (SD: 79) is redescribed by Hyppolite, whose subject is characterized by Butler as a tragic rather than a comic or heroic figure. Hyppolite's *Genesis and Structure of Hegel's 'Phenomenology of Spirit'* was published in France in 1946, following his translation of *Phenomenology* (1936–42), and Butler identifies the thrust of Hyppolite's argument as a retrospective historical rendering of the phenomenological 'narrative' charted by Hegel. As Butler puts it, 'only from a perspective beyond the *Phenomenology* do the historical origins of the text become clear', so that, as in Kojève's reading, the emphasis is on temporality and historicity (SD: 80). Like Kojève, Hyppolite questions the teleology of *Phenomenology*: significantly, rejecting the telos of the text also means rejecting the idea that 'the absolute' and 'being' are fixed and final, and being is seen as a process of 'becoming' through difference while the absolute is similarly open-ended and unfinished (SD: 84). Hyppolite thus privileges becoming over being, and desire is figured as an exchange between Self and Other rather than a violent confrontation. The Self recovers itself through its encounter with alterity or difference, and for Hyppolite the problem of desire and self-consciousness centres around the question of how to retain one's identity in the midst of alterity (SD: 89).

For Sartre, the final philosopher Butler considers in this section, coming into consciousness is a process of gradual *embodiment*. Whereas Kojève's desiring agents suffer from their physical 'abstractness' (i.e. their lack of physicality) (SD: 78), Butler characterizes Sartre's subject as 'an embodied and historically situated self' (SD: 93). Sartre gets around the problems of history and temporality encountered by Kojève's and Hyppolite's desiring subjects by suggesting that it is only through the imagination that desire can be satisfied (SD: 96). Butler writes that, for Sartre, '*human desire [is] a constant way of authoring imaginary worlds*' (SD: 97; her emphasis): writing is a non-finite activity, and this means that, like his predecessors, Sartre can reject the notion of a Hegelian unity resulting from the resolution of dialectic, and his existential agent makes this lack of unity and closure the subject matter of his texts and the basis of his literary form (SD: 98). For Sartre, desire is a process of textual self-creation and an opportunity to recognize freedom, and Butler claims that Sartre explores this theme in his own literary reconstructions of the French writers Jean Genet (1910–86) and Gustave Flaubert (1821–80). For Sartre, the desire for life as it is formulated in *Phenomenology* gives way to the desire to write the Self. The works of Flaubert and Genet represent the life of desire through their characters, and these works are themselves the products of desire, thus exemplifying the central question concerning desire and recognition in Sartre's *Being and Nothingness: An Essay in Phenomenological Ontology* (1943): is it possible to know another human, and to what extent is that human created in the knowing? (SD: 156).

DIFFÉRANCE AND PROLIFERATION

Focusing on two important essays by Foucault and Derrida, Butler brings to light what appears to be the unexpected 'Hegelian legacy' of these two philosophers: Foucault's essay 'Nietzsche, Genealogy, History' (1971) is characterized as a critique of a dialectical philosophy of history and a reworking of the Hegelian lordship and bondage relationship, while the essay that Derrida presented at Hyppolite's seminar, 'The Pit and the Pyramid: An Introduction to Hegel's Semiology' (1968), is a criticism of Hegel's theory of the sign.

To take the last-mentioned essay first. We have seen that difference is crucial to the Hegelian subject who must confront and overcome the Otherness of the Other in order to recognize himself. Derrida theorizes difference as *différance* in a linguistic context, a coinage which in French carries the dual meaning of both 'difference' and 'deferral'. Developing the theories of the Swiss linguist Ferdinand de Saussure (1857–1913), whose *Course in General Linguistics* (1916) is widely regarded as a basis for structuralist and post-structuralist theories, Derrida's concept of *différance* alludes to the way in which meaning is never present in itself but always depends on what is absent, so that it would be possible to say (as Derrida does) that in language there are only differences with no positive terms. Butler explains this in *Subjects*: 'Derrida concludes that the limits of signification, i.e. the "difference" of the sign from what it signifies, emerges time and again wherever language purports to cross the ontological rift between itself and a pure referent' (SD: 178). There is no such thing as a 'pure referent', a word that signifies in and of itself, since words only acquire meaning in relation to other words on the signifying chain (see box on p. 31).

According to Butler, Derrida's assertion that the sign fails to achieve completion constitutes a challenge to Hegel because it reveals that the subject's 'ambition' to achieve absolute being is an impossibility. If the subject is constructed in language, and if language as theorized by Derrida is incomplete and open-ended, then the subject *itself* will be similarly characterized by its incompletion (SD: 179). The contingency of Derrida's sign-in-progress does indeed resemble Hegel's subject-in-progress, that dialectical journeyer who only exists as the sum total of its travels past, present and future, with this crucial difference: Derrida's sign never reaches a point of absolute meaning or signifying, whereas we know that Hegel's subject is on a journey towards its ultimate destination, absolute knowledge.

If Derrida turns from Hegel to semiology (i.e. the theory of language as a system of signs) (SD: 179), for Foucault the turn is towards another philosopher, Friedrich Nietzsche (1844–1900), whose book *On the Genealogy of Morals* (1887) provides an alternative model of history and power to Hegel's. Butler describes Foucault's essay 'Nietzsche, Genealogy, History' as 'a Nietzschean reworking of the Hegelian scene' (SD: 180) in which Foucault both appropriates and rejects Hegelian dialectical strategies. Much of Foucault's work is concerned with theorizing forms of power and its deployment, and in 'Nietzsche, Genealogy, History' this is specifically linked to history and to modes of historicizing. Departing from Hegel's single scene of domination, Foucault characterizes power structures as pervasive rather than contained, generative rather than merely prohibitive. In other words, for Foucault, power does not emanate from a single or singular source, nor does it operate in a straightforwardly repressive manner. Likewise,

Foucault does not assume that history is unified in its origins and aims, but he characterizes it in terms of dissension, disparity and the struggle of forces (1971: 79). Dialectical unity will always be exceeded in this conflict with neither origin nor end, and Foucault's mode of historical analysis, or 'genealogy', explicitly seeks out difference and hetero-geneity in order to overthrow what Foucault calls 'the rancorous will to knowledge' (1971: 95).

It seems that both Derrida and Foucault have broken out of Hegelian dialectic, the former by affirming the multiplicity of the sign and the latter by affirming the multiplicity and excess of both power and history. For both thinkers, difference and disparity undermine any attempt to posit an identity, and Hegel's *Aufhebung*, the sublation of difference into sameness, is seen as a denial of difference and a strategy of concealment through which a fictive self-identical subject is posited (SD: 182). Does this constitute a 'break with Hegel', and could these two philosophers be described as 'post-Hegelian'? Butler affirms that using the prefix 'post-' and asserting a break with the past is in *itself* a dialectical move, so that 'references to a "break" with Hegel are almost always impossible, if only because Hegel has made the very notion of "breaking with" into the central tenet of his dialectic' (SD: 183–4). A non-dialectical break with Hegel would, she states, require that Foucault and Derrida find a way of being different from Hegel that could not be accounted for by his own thought and, in the second half of her chapter, Butler examines the further attempts to dismantle dialectical thinking through the 'death' of the Hegelian subject in Lacan, Deleuze and Foucault.

LOVE, LACK AND LANGUAGE

Like Derrida, Lacan talks about the subject in terms of its linguistic constitution so that, once again, the ontologically complete subject supposedly posited by Hegel is deemed to be an impossibility. In Lacan's account, it is only as an infant that the subject comes anywhere near to experiencing completion, since at this stage the subject is under no injunction to curb its incestuous desires. When 'the law of the father' imposes the taboo against incest, the infant is forced to repress its primary desires, necessitating the opening up of the unconscious as a repository for these urges. The paternal prohibition coincides with the child's entrance into language, in other words, the move from the pre-linguistic or imaginary to the linguistic or symbolic order. The incest taboo and the acquisition of language inaugurate an existence that from now on is characterized by lack, loss and the desire to regain those prohibited desires. As Butler puts it, the subject of desire is *the product of a prohibition* (SD: 187). This idea will prove to be crucial to her theorizations of gender, sex and sexuality in *Gender Trouble*.

It should be obvious that Lacan's subject, riven as it is by lack and impossible desires, is very different to the transparent, unfractured consciousness posited by Hegel. Once the unconscious has been acknowledged, it is impossible to think in terms of a self-identical coherent individual, since the subject is constituted by desires it cannot possibly know and cannot even speak, but which nonetheless determine its identity. All the same, Butler once again argues that Lacan is mischaracterizing Hegel's subject by ignoring its comedic unfinished nature and attributing self-transparency and completion to a subject that is in reality unfixed and *in*complete (SD: 196).

Both Deleuze and Foucault reject Lacan's characterization of the subject as defined by lack and loss, and his description of the law (in this case, the law of the father) as straightforwardly prohibitive. Butler points out that Deleuze sees desire as generative and productive rather than merely subject to prohibition, and in fact he regards Lacan's notion of desire-as-lack as an ideological product of capitalism designed to rationalize and maintain social and sexual oppression and existing hierarchies (SD: 206). Like Foucault, Deleuze also turns to Nietzsche in his rejection of what he sees as the implicit 'slave morality' of Hegelianism and the confrontation between the lord and his bondsman. By describing the subject as a Nietzschean *Übermensch* or 'super-person', Deleuze insists that the subject does not require this confrontation with its opposite in order to know itself, since the *Übermensch* is self-defined and not dependent on others. Like Foucault, Deleuze also sees power as a multiple, rather than singular, play of forces that cannot be contained by a dialectical unity (SD: 208–9).

Again, Butler argues that Deleuze has misread *Phenomenology* by overlooking the 'bacchanallian [*sic*] revel' and the 'celebratory conclusion' with which it ends (SD: 209). Moreover, in his rejection of Hegelian dialectic as anti-life, Butler claims that Deleuze characterizes desire as a brave force waiting be recovered and released, an idealistic view that ignores Lacan's insight that *all* desire is linguistically and culturally constructed and Foucault's parallel notion that there can be no insurrectionary desire that exists outside the terms of the law. Thus, according to Butler, 'both Lacan and Deleuze remain entranced by the metaphysical promise of desire as an immanent experience of the Absolute' (SD: 216).

Like Deleuze, Foucault acknowledges that the characterization of desire-as-lack is a cultural construction, but he argues that, far from requiring the intervention of a brave force from outside the law as a means of subversion, the law contains the possibility of subversion and proliferation within *itself*; specific examples of this will be considered in Chapter 2, 'Gender'. This is 'dialectics unmoored' (SD: 217), a strategic location of subversion within the law rather than in dialectical opposition to it. Butler argues that even Foucault's formulations of power as dispersed and polyvalent are dialectical because power still exists in relation to something, making Foucault, in Butler's view, 'a tenuous dialectician' whose dialectic has neither subject nor teleology. Although Foucault's work breaks out of a binary structure (SD: 225), Foucault *himself* constructs a binary by distinguishing between juridical and productive power, life and anti-life, and affirmation and negation. Similarly, Deleuze does the same by contrasting culturally-constructed desire-as-lack with a brave and self-defined Nietzschean desire waiting to be released. In spite of their attempts, it seems that none of these contemporary philosophers manages to avoid the philosophical structure of Hegelian dialectic. All the same, it is Foucault's theorizations of dialectic that most closely resemble the supplemented dialectic engaged by Butler in her own writing.

FORWARDS INTO HISTORY

It would seem that the four thinkers Butler examines in the final chapter of *Subjects of Desire* all remain within the terms of Hegelian dialectic, if only by virtue of their efforts to evade it, since any attempt to do so is an implicitly oppositional *dialectical* move. Moreover, it also appears that Derrida, Lacan, Deleuze and Foucault require the Hegelian subject as the basis for their conceptualizations of subjectivity; Butler remarks that 'it is striking to find how regularly even the most tenacious of post-Hegelians appear to remain faithful to the founding struggles of Hegel's desiring subject' (SD: 230) and she offers, via Kristeva, some concluding remarks as to a way forward for the post-Hegelian subject.

It might seem odd that Butler introduces a discussion of Kristeva's theories in the last few pages of *Subjects*, and her brief analysis of gender and the subject certainly has a 'last-minute' feel about it. (Butler draws out the implications of phenomenology for feminist theory and practice in two essays, 'Sexual Ideology and Phenomenological Description: A Feminist Critique of Merleau-Ponty's *Phenomenology of Perception*' (1989) and 'Performative Acts and Gender Constitution: An Essay in Phenomenology and Feminist Theory' (1997).) In fact, this is almost the first time Butler has raised the question of the gender of Hegel's subject, and here she cites Kristeva as the French reader who is most concerned to critique Hegel from a gendered perspective. According to Butler, the Kristevan body is 'a heterogenous assemblage of drives and needs', a theorization that automatically explodes the notion that body is a singular entity (SD: 232). Foucault and Kristeva both suggest that the Hegelian discourse on desire should give way to a discourse on bodies and, intriguingly, Butler identifies the critique of the desiring subject and the writing of a history of bodies as a future direction for philosophers that would signal what she calls 'the definitive closure of Hegel's narrative of desire' (although Butler's statement sounds like an attempt at dialectical resolution) (SD: 235).

Criticizing Foucault for the absence of an analysis of 'concrete bodies in complex historical situations' (SD: 237) Butler suggests that what is needed for a clearer, more specific understanding of desire is a history of bodies that does not reduce culture to the imposition of the law upon the body (SD: 238). All the same, her own study does not conclude with such a history (presumably because it is beyond the scope of *Subjects*), but with the somewhat unexpected reintroduction of the notion of the subject of desire as both constructed and comedic: 'From Hegel through Foucault, it appears that desire makes us into strangely fictive beings' she writes, 'And the laugh of recognition appears to be the occasion of insight' (SD: 238). It seems that it is only through parodic proliferation that dialectic will be dismantled, an idea that forms the basis of Butler's next major engagement with the subject in *Gender Trouble*.

SUMMARY

Subjects of Desire analyses the reception of G.W.F. Hegel's *Phenomenology of Spirit* by two generations of French philosophers. Hegel's Spirit progresses towards absolute knowledge by negating everything that comes in its way, overcoming obstacles in order to move on to the next stage in its development. Although the Spirit encounters numerous reversals, he is motivated to continue by his desire for recognition and self-consciousness. This can only take place through the overcoming of difference, which in turn involves the annihilation of the Other. The two generations of French philosophers who read *Phenomenology* tend to assume that Hegel's Spirit is self-identical and coherent, whereas Butler argues that these philosophers *construct* a version of Hegel's Spirit in order to depart from and supersede it in their formulations. Although these philosophers are attempting to break with Hegel, this discursive move remains within the structure of dialectic which involves negation (thesis – antithesis – synthesis).

Kojève's Marxist reading of *Phenomenology* attempts to break with Hegel by anticipating the end of history, and indeed the end of God, while Hyppolite characterizes Hegel's Absolute as an open-ended and unfinished process. Sartre suggests that the desire Hegel describes can only be satisfied imaginatively through art, and he claims that the existential agent makes lack of unity the subject-matter of his texts and the basis of his literary form.

The Hegelian subject is also interrogated by the next 'wave' of philosophers: for Lacan it is split, while for Derrida it is displaced and Foucault and Deleuze anticipate its eventual death. Towards the end of *Subjects*, Butler suggests via Foucault and Kristeva that the Hegelian discourse on desire must give way to a specific, historical account of the body. In two subsequent articles Butler argues that, although phenomenological writings such as those of Merleau-Ponty seem heteronormative, it is possible to rescue them for feminist analysis; to claim that existence is a sequence of 'acts' may undermine the idea that identities are pre-existing essences, an idea Butler develops in *Gender Trouble* and *Bodies That Matter*.

GENDER

FROM PHENOMENOLOGY TO 'FEMININITY'

Gender Trouble (1990; reissued 1999) is probably Butler's best-known work to date, and is widely regarded as her most important book. Butler's theorizations of performative identity have been described as the sine qua non (i.e. the indispensable condition) of postmodern feminism (Shildrick 1996), while others have argued that such ideas have pushed feminist theory into new terrain (McNay 1999: 175). Even thinkers who disagree with *Gender Trouble* would have to accept that it has been and continues to be influential and important in a wide range of fields.

How does Butler move from phenomenology to questions of 'femininity' and 'masculinity'? Does this constitute a break in her thought and a change of direction? And what is the result when a brilliant Hegelian turns her attention to current debates on sex, gender and sexuality? It would be a mistake to regard *Gender Trouble* as a radical departure from *Subjects of Desire*, and, although it would be equally mistaken to try to plot a straightforward progression in Butler's thought, it is important to be aware of the phenomenological and Hegelian threads running through all her work. Desire, recognition and alterity are still very much on Butler's mind in *Gender Trouble*, as is the constitution of the subject, the ways in which identity, and in particular *gender* identity, is constructed by and in discourse (SDII: xiv).

Gender Trouble is not a very long book (the text runs to about 150 pages) but its range of philosophical and theoretical reference is wide, and at times it may seem that you are expected to have a prior knowledge of the arguments and debates to which Butler is referring. Not only that, but you may find yourself struggling to follow a text whose basic theoretical premises can be difficult to grasp. Readers for whom 'Judith Butler' is synonymous with 'performativity' may well be tempted to skip straight to the relevant sections in both this chapter and *Gender Trouble* itself, but part of the reason Butler's theories have been misunderstood is precisely because they have been theoretically 'reduced' through decontextualization and simplification. It would make more sense to read *Gender Trouble* all the way through even if you find it difficult at first and, as with all the chapters in this book, you should not regard my accounts of Butler's theories as a substitute for reading the texts themselves.

Since Butler is such a syncretic (i.e. theoretically wide-ranging) writer, this chapter will not be able to offer detailed discussions of all the thinkers and theories from which Butler draws, but instead will focus on a number of *Gender Trouble*'s key theoretical formulations: namely, the Foucauldian critique of the subject, Butler's readings of structuralist, psychoanalytic and feminist theories, and her own theorizations of melancholic and performative identities. At this stage, terms such as Foucauldianism, melancholia and performativity may be unfamiliar to you, but they will be explained in the sections below.

(WHERE) IS THERE A SUBJECT IN THIS TEXT?

Asserting that many feminist theorists have mistakenly assumed the existence of 'the subject' by talking uncritically in terms of 'woman' and 'women', *Gender Trouble* calls the existence of this category into question. Rather than starting from the premise that the subject is a pre-existing metaphysical journeyer, Butler describes it as a subject-in-process that is constructed in discourse by the acts it performs.

Gender Trouble makes trouble by:

- calling the category of 'the subject' into question by arguing that it is a performative construct; and

- asserting that there are ways of 'doing' one's identity which will cause even further trouble for those who have a vested interest in preserving existing oppositions such as male/female, masculine/feminine, gay/straight and so on (Butler does not deal with black/white in *Gender Trouble*).

The idea that identity is a performative construct is a complex theory that will be analyzed in detail below, but at this stage you should note that it would be incorrect to assume that, if Hegel's Spirit is a traveller (see previous chapter), Butler's subject is an actor that simply gets up and 'performs' its identity on a metaphorical stage of its own choosing. As we shall see, Butler does claim that gender identity is a sequence of acts (an idea that has existential underpinnings), but she also argues that there is no pre-existing performer who does those acts, no doer behind the deed. Here she draws a distinction between *performance* (which presupposes the existence of a subject) and *performativity* (which does not). This does not mean that there is no subject, but that the subject is not exactly where we would expect to find it – i.e. 'behind' or 'before' its deeds – so that reading *Gender Trouble* will call for new and radical ways of looking at (or perhaps looking *for*) gender identity.

'WOMAN' AS A TERM IN PROCESS

In *The Second Sex,* de Beauvoir famously claims that 'One is not born, but rather becomes, a woman. No biological, psychological, or economic fate determines the figure that the human female presents in society; it is civilisation as a whole that produces this creature, inter-mediate between male and eunuch, which is described as feminine' (1949: 281). Commenting on de Beauvoir's statement towards the end of the first chapter of *Gender Trouble*, Butler writes:

> If there is something right in Beauvoir's claim that one is not born, but rather *becomes* a woman, it follows that *woman* itself is a term in process, a becoming, a constructing that cannot rightfully be said to originate or to end. As an ongoing discursive practice, it is open to intervention and resig-nification. Even when gender seems to congeal into the most reified forms, the 'congealing' is itself an insistent and insidious practice, sustained and regulated by various social means. It is, for Beauvoir, never possible finally

to become a woman, as if there were a *telos* that governs the process of accul-
turation and construction.

(GT: 33)

Gender Trouble describes how gender 'congeals' or solidifies into a form
that makes it appear to have been there all along, and both Butler and
de Beauvoir assert that gender is a process which has neither origin nor
end, so that it is something that we 'do' rather than 'are'. In her early
article, 'Sex and Gender in Simone de Beauvoir's *Second Sex*', Butler
declares that 'all gender is, by definition, unnatural' before she proceeds
to unprise sex and gender from what many would assume to be their
inevitable connection to each other (SG: 35). Butler departs from the
common assumption that sex, gender and sexuality exist in relation to
each other, so that if, for example, one is biologically female, one is
expected to display 'feminine' traits and (in a heteronormative world,
i.e. a world in which heterosexuality is deemed to be the norm) to
desire men. Instead Butler claims that gender is 'unnatural', so that
there is no necessary relationship between one's body and one's gender. In that case, it will be possible to have a designated 'female' body
and *not* to display traits generally considered 'feminine': in other words,
one may be a 'masculine' female or a 'feminine' male. In the first chapter of *Gender Trouble*, Butler develops this idea by arguing that 'sex by
definition, will be shown to have been gender all along' (GT: 8), an idea
that will be discussed in detail later in this chapter.

Butler's article and the opening chapter of *Gender Trouble* raise a
number of important questions. If gender is a process or a 'becoming'
rather than an ontological state of being that one simply 'is', then what
determines what we become, as well as the *way* in which we become
it? To what extent does one choose one's gender? Indeed, what or
who is it that is doing the choosing, and what if anything determines
that choice? In another early article, 'Variations on Sex and Gender:
Beauvoir, Wittig and Foucault', Butler claims that gender is a 'choice'
(VSG: 128–9), an idea that is not quite as straightforward as it might
appear, since by 'choice' Butler does *not* mean that a 'free agent' or
'person' stands outside its gender and simply selects it. This would be
impossible, since one is *already* one's gender and one's choice of
'gender style' is always limited from the start. Instead, Butler asserts
that '[t]o choose a gender is to interpret received gender norms in a
way that organizes them anew. Less a radical act of creation, gender

is a tacit project to renew one's cultural history in one's own terms. This is not a prescriptive task we must endeavor to do, but one in which we have been endeavoring all along' (VSG: 131).

What Butler means is that gender is an act or a sequence of acts that is always and inevitably occurring, since it is impossible to exist as a social agent outside the terms of gender. *Gender Trouble* will place gender and sex in the context of the discourses by which it is framed and formed, so that the constructed (as opposed to the 'natural') character of both categories will be revealed. Butler embarks on her radical critique in the first chapter of *Gender Trouble* where she departs from theorists such as Wittig and Irigaray by arguing that there is no 'single or abiding ground' from which feminism can or should speak. These, she claims, are exclusionary practices which paradoxically undermine the feminist project to broaden the field of representation (GT: 5).

DISCOURSE

When Butler uses this word she is not just referring to 'speaking' or 'conversation', but specifically to Foucault's formulations of discourse as 'large groups of statements' governing the way we speak about and perceive a specific historical moment or moments. Foucault understands statements as repeatable events that are connected by their historical contexts, and his work seeks out the continuities between statements that together make up discursive formations such as 'medicine', 'criminality', 'madness'. In particular, Foucault is interested in the subject positions presupposed by utterances, and the way in which subjects are discursively constituted. So in *Madness and Civilisation* (1961) Foucault claims that the concept of mental illness was constructed in the nineteenth century, while in *The History of Sexuality Vol. I* (1976), he argues that sex and sexuality were simultaneously controlled and produced in a discursive explosion which took place in the nineteenth century. In other words, concepts such as 'madness', 'criminality' and 'sexuality' are discursive constructs which should be analyzed in the context of the specific historical context or shift in which they occurred.

Butler rejects such essentialism, even as a political strategy (GT: 4). A far more effective mode of contesting the status quo will be to *displace* categories such as 'man', 'woman', 'male' and 'female' by revealing how they are discursively constructed within a heterosexual matrix of power (GT: 30). While Wittig claims that lesbian is a concept that is beyond the categories of sex and calls for the destruction of heterosexuality as a social system (1992: 20), Butler argues that sex and gender are discursively constructed and that there is no such position of implied freedom beyond discourse. Culturally constructed sexuality cannot be repudiated, so that the subject is left with the question of how to acknowledge and 'do' the construction it is already in (GT: 31). *Gender Trouble* will describe how genders and sexes are currently 'done' within the heterosexual matrix, while elaborating on how it is possible to 'do' those constructions differently.

GENDER GENEALOGIES

Asserting that gender constructions 'congeal' into forms which appear to be natural and permanent, Butler sets herself the task of desolidifying or deconstructing those forms by enquiring into how 'woman' came to be so widely accepted as an ontological given. At the beginning of *Gender Trouble* she asserts that feminist critique should analyze how the category 'women' is produced and restrained by power structures, rather than looking to those power structures for emancipation (GT: 2). Rather than engaging in a critique of 'patriarchy', Butler embarks upon what she calls '*a feminist genealogy* of the category of women' (GT: 5; her emphasis), and 'a genealogy of gender ontology' (GT: 32). The word 'genealogy' might seem to promise the historical analysis towards which Butler gestures as a future direction for philosophy at the end of *Subjects of Desire*, but in *Gender Trouble* she uses the word in its specifically Foucauldian sense to mean an investigation into how discourses function and the political aims they fulfil (see p. 10 for a definition). As she puts it, 'genealogy investigates the political stakes in designating as an *origin* and *cause* those identity categories that are in fact the *effects* of institutions, practices, discourses, with multiple and diffused points of origin' (GT: viii–ix; her emphasis). It will be useful to bear this sentence in mind as you read, since the idea that the subject is an *effect* rather than a cause is the key to Butler's theories of performative identity.

Accordingly, Butler is not interested in tracing gender back to its origin or cause (since it does not have one), but a genealogical investigation will study the effects of gender and will assume that gender *is* an effect. At this stage Butler's effect–cause formulation might seem back-to-front, but the idea will be explained in more detail later in this chapter when we return to Butler's theories of performativity.

SEX IS GENDER

If we accept that gender is constructed and that it is not in any way 'naturally' or inevitably connected to sex, then the distinction between sex and gender comes to seem increasingly unstable. In that case, gender is radically independent of sex, 'a free-floating artifice' as Butler puts it (GT: 6), raising the question as to whether 'sex' is as culturally constructed as gender; indeed, perhaps sex was always already gender, so that the sex/gender distinction is actually not a distinction at all (GT: 7). Butler dispenses with the idea that either gender *or* sex is an 'abiding substance' by arguing that a heterosexual, heterosexist culture establishes the coherence of those categories in order to perpetuate and maintain what the feminist poet and critic Adrienne Rich has called 'compulsory heterosexuality' – the dominant order in which men and women are required or even forced to be heterosexual. Butler claims that gender identities that do not conform to the system of 'compulsory and naturalized heterosexuality' expose how gender norms are socially instituted and maintained (GT: 22). As an example she cites Herculine Barbin, a nineteenth-century hermaphrodite who is uncategorizable within the terms of a heterosexual gender binary which assumes a simple correlation between sex and gender and divides people neatly into male/female, masculine/feminine. The twentieth-century English edition of Barbin's journals (Barbin 1980) is introduced by Foucault and, although Butler departs from Foucault's account of Herculine's experience in significant ways, she nonetheless affirms that the sexual heterogeneity that is literally *embodied* by Herculine constitutes an implicit critique of what Butler calls 'the metaphysics of substance' and 'the identitarian categories of sex' (GT: 23–4).

'Metaphysics of substance' refers to the pervasive belief that sex and the body are self-evidently 'natural' *material* entities, whereas we shall see that, for Butler, sex and gender are 'phantasmatic' cultural constructions which contour and define the body. Butler argues that Barbin's failure to conform to gender binarisms reveals the instability of those categories, calling into question gender as a substance and the viability of 'man' and 'woman' as nouns (GT: 24). Gender dissonance, or indeed gender trouble as exemplified by Barbin, demonstrates that gender is a fictive production (GT: 24), leading Butler to assert that *'gender* is not a noun [but it] proves to be performative, that is, constituting the identity it is purported to be. In this sense, gender is always a doing, though not a doing by a subject who might be said to preexist the deed' (GT: 25). This is one of Butler's most influential and difficult ideas, and it will be discussed in the sections that follow.

OUT OF THE CLOSET

Although Butler asserts that gender is constrained by the power structures within which it is located, she also insists on the possibilities for proliferation and subversion from within those constraints. To describe gender as a 'doing' and a corporeal style might lead you to think of it as an activity that resembles choosing an outfit from an already-existing wardrobe of clothes. Although Butler explicitly refutes this analogy in her next book, *Bodies That Matter*, it may serve our purposes for the time being. To start with, we will clearly have to do away with the notion of 'freedom of choice': since you are living within the law or within a given culture, there is no sense in which your choice is entirely 'free', and it is very likely that you 'choose' your metaphorical clothes to suit the expectations or perhaps the demands of your peers or your work colleagues, even if you don't realize that you are doing so. Furthermore, the range of clothes available to you will be determined by factors such as your culture, your job, your income and your social background/status.

In Butler's scheme of things, if you decided to ignore the expectations and the constraints imposed by your peers, colleagues, etc. by 'putting on a gender', which for some reason would upset those people who have authority over you or whose approval you require, you could not simply *reinvent* your metaphorical gender wardrobe or acquire an entirely new one (and even if you could do that, you would obviously be limited by what was available in the shops). Rather, you would have to alter the clothes you already have in order to signal that you are not wearing them in a 'conventional' way – by ripping them or sewing sequins on them or wearing them back to front or upside down. In other words, your choice of gender is curtailed, as is your choice of subversion – which might make it seem as though what you are doing is not 'choosing' or 'subverting' your gender at all.

The analogy is somewhat crude, but it will give you an idea of the ways in which our gender choices are limited rather than 'free'. Moreover, this model of gender identity raises questions about *agency* (i.e. choice and action) and the agent: if we compare gender to choosing an outfit from a limited wardrobe, then once again we must ask who or what is doing the choosing? My example of a person who stands in front of a wardrobe of clothes and chooses what to wear that day, implies the existence of a subject or an agent that is *prior* to gender (or putting on clothes in this example). As we shall see, this is an idea that Butler rejects in *Gender Trouble*, where the notion of gender as performative does not assume that there is an 'actor' pre-existing the acts which effectively constitute identity.

FOUNDATIONALIST FICTIONS

Although Butler is widely known for her formulations of performativity, parody and drag as outlined in the third chapter of *Gender Trouble*, the second chapter, 'Prohibition, Psychoanalysis, and the Production of the Heterosexual Matrix', is crucial to understanding Butler's models of identity. Reading structuralist and psychoanalytic accounts of gender, identity and the law through a Foucauldian lens Butler

- gives what she calls 'a discursive account of the cultural production of gender'; in other words, she works from the premise that gender is a discursive construct, something that is *produced*, and not a 'natural fact'; and
- characterizes the law as multiple, proliferating and potentially self-subverting as opposed to the singular, prohibitive and rigidly repressive law posited by other theorists (for example, Lacan).

The key words in Butler's chapter title are *production* and *matrix*. A dictionary will tell you that the word 'matrix' has several meanings: a mould in which something is cast or shaped; a womb; or, in computing, a grid-like array of interconnected circuit elements. It is difficult to tell in precisely which sense Butler is using the word, but, since it is unlikely that she thinks of gender as a womb, it would appear that the first and the third definitions apply here. In that case, gender could be characterized as a 'structure', a 'mould' or a 'grid' in which (or by which) the subject is 'cast' (although it is also important to bear in mind that the matrix is *itself* produced and consolidated by the theories Butler discusses here).

The chapter begins with a discussion of the analyses of structures of kinship by the structuralist anthropologist Claude Lévi-Strauss (1908–), before going on to analyze the psychoanalytic formulations of Lacan, Joan Riviere (1883–1962) and Freud. Butler then offers her own account of gender/sexual identity and the law via the theories of contemporary post-Freudian psychoanalysts, Nicolas Abraham and Maria Torok, and the post-structuralist, Foucault. I shall spend some time analyzing Freud's important theories of identity formation, but space will not permit a detailed analysis of the other thinkers whose work Butler critiques. Many of the theories we will be touching on are complex and do not lend themselves easily to summary, and you might find it useful to cross-refer with other books in the *Routledge Critical Thinkers* series (for example, Pamela Thurschwell's *Sigmund Freud* (2000), especially the third chapter, 'Sexuality') or to consult introductory accounts of critical theory, psychoanalysis and feminism (see 'Further Reading').

MOURNING AND MELANCHOLIA

Since Butler's theories are so heavily inflected by Freud's, in the following sections it will be necessary to explain a number of key Freudian concepts. Butler's readings of Freud are complex and difficult to understand in places, partly because of Freud's apparent uncertainties and the frequent emendations he made to his theories, and partly because it is not always clear from which of Freud's theories Butler is drawing, or if indeed she is drawing from them at all. Butler makes use of two important works by Freud, 'Mourning and Melancholia' and the later *The Ego and the Id*. In 'Mourning and Melancholia' Freud distinguishes between *mourning*, which is the reaction to a real loss, usually the death of a loved one, and *melancholia*. Since the melancholic does not always know what he or she has lost and is in fact sometimes unaware of having 'lost' anything at all, Freud regards it as a pathological condition resembling depression. He argues that, instead of 'getting over' and accepting the loss, the melancholic response is to take the lost object into the ego by *identifying* with it.

Identification is a concept that is central to Freud's theories of the structuring of the mind into ego, superego and id and, as you might expect, denotes the process and effects of identifying with others, often as a response to loss. *Introjection* is the process whereby the subject takes objects from the outside world into itself and preserves them in the ego, and is closely related to identification. In fact, identification takes place through introjection as an object is metaphorically 'installed' in the ego, and Butler will argue that introjection is not the only way in which identification takes place.

In *The Ego and the Id* Freud no longer regards melancholia as a pathology or mental illness, but he now describes all ego formation as a melancholic structure. Freud claims that in the process of ego-formation a child's primary object-cathexes are transformed into an identification, a formulation that is not as complicated as it might sound once you have deciphered the Freudian terminology. Initially the infant desires one or other of its parents (these are its primary object-cathexes), but the taboo against incest means that these desires have to be given up. Like the melancholic who takes the lost object into her- or himself and thereby preserves it, the ego introjects the lost object (the desired parent) and preserves it as an identification. '[A]n object which was lost has been set up again inside the ego – that is . . . an object-cathexis has been replaced by an identification', Freud writes (1923: 367). The ego is therefore a repository of all the desires it has had to give up, or as Freud puts it, 'the character of the ego is a precipitate of abandoned object-cathexes and . . . it contains the history of those object-choices' (1923: 368).

FREUD: USEFUL TERMS

Mourning: the response to a real loss.

Melancholia: the response to an imagined loss.

Object-cathexis: the desire for an object; in this case, one's mother or father.

Identification: the process by which one comes to identify with someone or something; in this context, the object that has been lost. Identifications take place through *introjection* or *incorporation*.

Introjection: the process whereby objects from the outside world are taken into and preserved in the ego.

Incorporation:	the process whereby objects are preserved on the surface of the body (Freud does not discuss incorporation in 'Mourning and Melancholia' or *The Ego and the Id*).
Dispositions:	whether, from birth onwards, you desire members of the same or the opposite sex.

If your primary desire is for your mother, you will introject the figure of your mother and establish an identification with her; conversely, if your primary desire is for your father, you will substitute your impermissible object-cathexis for an identification with him. Freud is not sure what determines the primary object-cathexis – i.e. why the infant desires one parent rather than the other – but he gets around this problem by attributing the direction of the infant's desire to what he calls *dispositions*. By 'disposition' he appears to mean the infant's innate desire for a member of the opposite or the same sex, but Freud expresses some hesitation on this subject in his description of the development of the 'little girl'. Freud writes that, after relinquishing her father as a primary love-object, the girl 'will bring her masculinity into prominence and identify with her father (that is, with the object that has been lost) instead of with her mother. This will clearly depend on whether the masculinity in her disposition – whatever that may consist in – is strong enough [i.e. to identify with her father]' (1923: 372). It would seem that object-cathexes are the result of primary dispositions, i.e. whether one is innately 'masculine' or 'feminine' to start with, and, as you might expect by now, Butler refutes Freud's somewhat tentative postulation of innate sexual 'dispositions'.

MELANCHOLIC HETEROSEXUALITY

Now let us look at what Butler does with Freud. Butler is interested in the 'dispositions' Freud glosses over somewhat hastily, but, rather than accepting that they are innate, she wants to know how 'masculine' and 'feminine' dispositions can be traced to an identification, and where those identifications take place. In fact, Butler asserts that dispositions are the *effects* of identifications with the parent of the same/opposite sex rather than the *causes* of those identifications; in other words, desire does not come first. 'What are these primary dispositions on which Freud himself apparently founders?' she asks, noting the 'hyphenated doubt' ('– whatever that may consist in –') with which he interrupts his assertion (GT: 60).

While Freud describes ego formation as a melancholic structure because the infant is forced to give up its desire for its parents in response to the taboo against incest, Butler argues that the taboo against incest is *preceded* by the taboo against homosexuality (although curiously, she does not specify her source here) (GT: 63). This seems to imply that the child's primary desire is always for the parent of the same sex – after all, why do you need a taboo if there is nothing to prohibit? – and although Butler argues that the law *produces* the desire it subsequently prohibits, she is still unspecific as to why one desire is produced and repressed before another. 'Although Freud does not explicitly argue in its favour, it would appear that the taboo against homosexuality must *precede* the heterosexual incest taboo', writes Butler (GT: 64) and, although she reiterates this assertion several times in this section, the qualifiers she introduces here ('Although Freud', 'it would appear') resemble the 'hyphenated doubt' that she notes in Freud's description of dispositions.

All the same, the assertion that the taboo against homosexuality precedes the incest taboo is crucial to Butler's argument that gender and sex identities are formed in response to prohibition. Rather than regarding gender or sex as innate, Butler asserts that 'gender identity appears primarily to be the internalization of a prohibition that proves to be formative of identity' (GT: 63). Since the 'prohibition' to which Butler refers is the taboo against homosexuality, it is clear that for Butler all gender identity is founded on a primary, forbidden homosexual cathexis or desire. If melancholia is the response to real or imagined loss, and if heterosexual gender identity is formed on the basis of the primary loss of the same-sexed object of desire, it follows that heterosexual gender identity is melancholic.

Butler's Foucauldian appropriation of Freud's theories of mourning, melancholia and ego formation and her argument that heterosexuality is founded on primary homosexual desire constitute one of *Gender Trouble*'s most important achievements and, since the theory of melancholic gender identities and identifications underscores so much of her subsequent work, I will quote Butler at length here by way of summary:

> If feminine and masculine dispositions are the result of the effective internalization of [the taboo against homosexuality], and if the melancholic answer to

the loss of the same-sexed object is to incorporate and, indeed, *to become* that object through the construction of the ego-ideal, then gender identity appears primarily to be the internalization of a prohibition that proves to be formative of identity. Further, this identity is constructed and maintained by the consistent application of this taboo, not only in the stylization of the body in compliance with discrete categories of sex but in the production and 'disposition' of sexual desire . . . dispositions are not the primary sexual facts of the psyche, but produced effects of a law imposed by culture and by the complicitous and transvaluating acts of the ego ideal.

(GT: 63–4)

You may have noticed the word 'incorporate' in the section I have just quoted and, although you will not find the word in the index of *Gender Trouble*, 'incorporation' is a crucial component of Butler's arguments concerning gender, sex and the body.

MELANCHOLY HETEROSEXUALITY

The case study of the 'little girl' could be summarized as follows: 'little girl's' desire for her mother → incest taboo → 'little girl's' melancholia → identification with mother through incorporation → 'little girl's' disavowed homosexual desire → femininity → melancholic heterosexuality.

INCORPORATION

By referring to 'the stylization of the body' and 'the production and "disposition" of sexual desire' in the section I have just quoted, Butler introduces the idea that sex, as much as gender, is a result of the taboo against homosexuality. So far she has argued that the taboo against homosexuality triggers the melancholic response described by Freud in 'Mourning and Melancholia', in other words, an identification with the parent of the same sex. Butler talks of this identification in terms of 'internalization', implying that, as in Freud's descriptions, the lost object is introjected and set up in the ego as an identification. Now, departing from Freud, who does not talk about incorporation in 'Mourning and Melancholia' or *The Ego and the Id*, Butler asks *where* melancholic identification takes place, and she concludes that identifications are incorporated, i.e. preserved on the surface of the body

(GT: 67). Here Butler follows Abraham and Torok, who argue that, whereas mourning leads to the introjection of the lost object, melancholia results in its incorporation. 'When we consider gender identity as a melancholic structure, it makes sense to choose "incorporation" as the manner by which that identification is accomplished', Butler writes; '[G]ender identity would be established through a refusal of loss that encrypts itself in the body . . . incorporation *literalizes* the loss *on* or *in* the body and so appears as the facticity of the body, the means by which the body comes to bear "sex" as its literal truth' (GT: 68).

It is not just the ego that is the receptacle for object-cathexes that have had to be abandoned, but the body itself is a sort of 'tomb' (note the word 'encrypts') in which, however, these lost desires are far from 'buried' since they are preserved on the surface of the body and thus constitute one's sex and gender identities. Butler formulates the onto-logical equation in the following way: 'If the heterosexual denial of homosexuality results in melancholia and if melancholia operates through incorporation, then the disavowed homosexual love is preserved through the cultivation of an oppositionally defined gender identity' (GT: 69). Or, more bluntly put, you *are* what you have desired (and are no longer permitted to desire).

All stable gender identities are 'melancholic', founded on a prohib-ited primary desire that is written on the body and, as Butler asserts, rigid gender boundaries conceal the loss of an original, unacknowl-edged and unresolved love (GT: 63). It is not just straight people who suffer from melancholy gender (if 'suffer' is the right verb: Butler calls melancholy heterosexuality a 'syndrome', which does seem to hint that there is something pathological about it (GT: 71)). Butler accepts that 'a homosexual for whom heterosexual desire is unthink-able' will maintain his or her heterosexual desire through the melancholic incorporation of that desire, but she points out that, since there is not the same cultural sanction against acknowledging hetero-sexuality, heterosexual and homosexual melancholia are not really equivalent (GT: 70).

Like gender, the body conceals its genealogy and presents itself as a 'natural fact' or a given, whereas, by arguing that relinquished desire is 'encrypted' on the body, Butler asserts that the body is the effect of desire rather than its cause. The body is an imagined structure which is the consequence or the product of desire: 'the phantasmatic nature of desire reveals the body not as its ground or cause, but as its *occasion* and its *object*', she writes; 'The strategy of desire is in part the transfiguration of the desiring body itself' (GT: 71). The idea that desire 'transfigures' the body is complex, but for the purposes of this discussion it is enough to note that Butler is not positing a body that is stable, fixed and 'merely matter', but one that is constructed and contoured by discourse and the law. Butler returns to the question of the body in the third chapter of *Gender Trouble*, 'Subversive Bodily Acts', where she considers both sex and gender as 'enactments' that operate performatively to establish the appearance of bodily fixity.

If both gender and sex are 'enactments' rather than givens, then it will be possible to enact them in unexpected, potentially subversive ways. Before she goes on to discuss performativity and parody, Butler considers the subversive potential of the law.

MELANCHOLY GENDER

The loss of a love object results in melancholy and an identification with that object. According to Butler, the taboo against homosexuality precedes the taboo against incest, which means that homosexual desire is prohibited from the outset. Whereas it is possible to grieve the consequences of the incest taboo in a heterosexual culture, the taboo against homosexuality cannot be grieved and so the response to the taboo against homosexuality is melancholia rather than mourning (GT: 69).

The melancholic identification with same-sexed parent is incorporated, i.e. preserved on the surface of the body, so that, far from being 'natural' or a given, like gender, sex is a process, something one assumes through identification and incorporation. The melancholy heterosexual subject will 'bear' her or his forbidden same-sex desire on the surface of the body, so that physical 'ultra-femininity' and 'ultra-masculinity' denote the subject's relinquished desire for an object of the same sex. This means that you 'are' what you have desired, and that the desires you have been prevented from expressing are symptomatized on the body and in your behaviour.

All sexuality and gender identities are melancholic, but Butler points out that, since there is not the same sanction against acknowledging heterosexual desire in a heterosexual culture, homosexual and heterosexual melancholia are not identical.

PROLIFERATION AS POWER

The structuralist and psychoanalytic theories that Butler subjects to genealogical analysis assume that sex and gender are universal, stable and innate. Butler, on the other hand, emphasizes that sex and gender are the results of discourse and the law, and towards the end of the long second chapter she emphasizes the plurality of a law which *produces* sexed and gendered identities that are presented as innate and 'natural' before they are subjected to prohibition. While she does not dispute Lévi-Strauss' and Freud's assumption that sexed and gendered identities are the products of laws and taboos, Butler departs from these theorists by claiming that the law produces the inadmissible identities and desires it represses in order to establish and maintain the stability of sanctioned sex and gender identities.

Here Butler is deploying *the critique of the repressive hypothesis* as formulated by Foucault, who refutes the common assumption that sexuality in the nineteenth century was repressed by the law. Instead he argues that sexuality was *produced* by the law and that, far from keeping silent about sex, in the nineteenth century there was 'a multi-plication of discourses concerning sex in the field of exercise of power itself; an institutional incitement to speak about it, and to do so more and more' (Foucault 1976: 18). Foucault claims that speaking about sex is a way of simultaneously producing and controlling it, and he also argues that, since there is no position that can be taken up outside the law, subversion must occur *within* existing discursive structures.

Foucault's critique of the repressive hypothesis leads Butler to argue that the law which prohibits homosexual/incestuous unions simulta-neously invents and invites them. Butler accordingly insists on 'the generativity of [the incest] taboo . . . [N]ot only does the taboo forbid and dictate sexuality in certain forms, but it inadvertently produces a variety of substitute desires and identities that are in no sense constrained in advance, except insofar as they are "substitutes" in some sense' (GT: 76). This means that it is impossible to separate the repressive and the productive function of both the taboo against homosexuality and the taboo against incest, since the law *itself* both prohibits and produces desire for one's parents and same-sex desire.

Butler acknowledges that psychoanalysis has always recognized the productive function of the incest taboo, and her application of the same argument to the taboo against homosexuality leads her to conclude that heterosexuality *requires* homosexuality in order to define itself and maintain its stability. '[H]omosexuality emerges as a desire which must be produced in order to remain repressed', she writes; heterosexuality produces intelligible homosexuality and then renders it unintelligible by prohibiting it (GT: 77).

The idea that homosexuality is 'produced' in order to maintain the coherence of heterosexuality is attractive but problematic, since it risks pathologizing homosexuality and consigning it to a secondary position in relation to heterosexuality – a product of a heterosexualizing law. (Jonathan Dollimore makes a similar point when he argues that 'reading Butler one occasionally gets the impression that gay desire is not complete unless it is somehow installed subversively inside heterosexuality' (1996: 535). You might also wonder whether this formulation contradicts Butler's assertion that the taboo against homosexuality *precedes* the taboo against incest, since this might imply that homosexual desire precedes heterosexual desire. Here it seems that Butler's earlier line of causation has been reversed, since homosexuality is now characterized as a secondary discursive formation that is produced in order to establish the stability of heterosexuality. This apparent contradiction may be the result of a potential incompatibility between psychoanalysis (which is concerned with the origins of identity) and Foucauldian theory (which is not). Moreover, it could be argued that Butler's characterization of sexual identities as melancholic responses to the taboos against homosexuality and incest resembles the Lacanian formulations that she rejected in *Subjects of Desire*, namely, Lacan's idea that the subject is constituted by lack and loss (of desire) and that it is in thrall to 'the law of the father'.

And yet, unlike Lacan, Butler insists that the law is generative and plural, and that subversion, parody and drag occur *within* a law that provides opportunities for the 'staging' of the subversive identities that it simultaneously suppresses and produces.

BODIES IN THEORY

Throughout *Gender Trouble* Butler makes numerous allusions to performativity, but she gives her most sustained elucidation of the theory in a surprisingly (given its influence) brief section towards the end of the third chapter (GT: 136–41). It is significant that this theory has overshadowed the rest of *Gender Trouble*, and I risk compounding this by focusing on performativity in the two sections that follow. It is unfortunate that we will have to gloss over the thinkers and theories that lead Butler to her formulations of performativity, but the brief survey that follows will hopefully assist your own reading of this chapter of *Gender Trouble*.

Butler's discussions of Kristeva, Foucault and Wittig focus on their descriptions of the body: whereas both Kristeva and, at times, Foucault assume that there is a body prior to discourse, Butler follows Wittig, the materialist lesbian theorist, in asserting that morphology, i.e. the form of the body, is the product of a heterosexual scheme (or, as before, a 'matrix') that effectively contours that body. Like gender, sex is an *effect*, a discursive category that, as Butler puts it, 'imposes an artificial unity on an otherwise discontinuous set of attributes' (GT: 114), an idea that we came across in the previous section. Here Butler endorses the statement that Wittig makes in two of the essays in her collection *The Straight Mind*, where she writes that 'language casts sheaves of reality upon the social body, stamping it and violently shaping it' (1992: 43–4, 78). Wittig's statement might seem to imply that there is a body which pre-exists language (after all, language must have something to cast its 'sheaves' upon) but Butler calls such an assumption into question when she asks: 'Is there a "physical" body prior to the perceptually perceived body? An impossible question to decide' (GT: 114).

Butler returns to this 'impossible question' in *Bodies That Matter* where she more or less accepts that there is such a thing as the 'physical body', the thing that hurts if you kick it and bleeds if you prick it, but in this section of *Gender Trouble* she discusses how perception and the body are discursively constructed through exclusion, taboo and abjection (the last is a Kristevan term). One of the exclusionary discourses Butler analyzes is 'science', and in a brief section entitled 'Concluding Unscientific Postscript' which is somewhat surreptitiously tucked away between her discussion of Foucault and her discussion of Wittig, Butler discusses some recent, (albeit rather unspecific) 'scientific' advances in cell biology. '[A] good ten per cent of the population has chromosomal variations that do not fit neatly into the XX-female and XY-male set of categories', Butler claims, a 'fact' that leads her to suggest that existing sex/gender binaries are inadequate for the task of describing and categorizing indeterminate bodies. Rather than simply accepting the authority of 'science', subjecting cell biology to discursive analysis reveals that science itself is determined by the heterosexual matrix, or, as Butler puts it, 'that cultural assumptions regarding the relative status of men and women and the binary relation of gender itself frame and focus the research into sex-determination' (GT: 109).

'Science' and 'naturalness' are discursive constructs (see p. 47) and, although it might seem strange to refute the authority of 'science' after quoting apparently 'scientific' data, the point Butler is making is clear: the body is not a 'mute facticity' (GT: 129), i.e. a fact of nature, but like gender it is produced by discourses such as the ones Butler has been analyzing. As with gender, to suggest that there is no body prior to cultural inscription will lead Butler to argue that sex as well as gender can be performatively reinscribed in ways that accentuate its factitious-ness (i.e. its constructedness) rather than its facticity (i.e. the fact of its existence). Such reinscriptions, or re-citations as Butler will call them in *Bodies That Matter*, constitute the subject's agency within the law, in other words, the possibilities of subverting the law against itself. Agency is an important concept for Butler, since it signifies the opportunities for subverting the law against itself to radical, political ends.

PERFORMATIVITY

Butler has collapsed the sex/gender distinction in order to argue that there is no sex that is not always already gender. All bodies are gendered from the beginning of their social existence (and there is no existence that is not social), which means that there is no 'natural body' that pre-exists its cultural inscription. This seems to point towards the conclusion that gender is not something one *is*, it is some-thing one *does*, an act, or more precisely, a sequence of acts, a verb rather than a noun, a 'doing' rather than a 'being' (GT: 25). Butler elaborates this idea in the first chapter of *Gender Trouble*:

> Gender is the repeated stylization of the body, a set of repeated acts within a highly rigid regulatory frame that congeal over time to produce the appear-ance of substance, of a natural sort of being. A political genealogy of gender ontologies, if it is successful, will deconstruct the substantive appearance of gender into its constitutive acts and locate and account for those acts within the compulsory frames set by the various forces that police the social appear-ance of gender.

(GT: 33)

Gender is not just a process, but it is a particular type of process, 'a set of repeated acts *within a highly rigid regulatory frame*' as Butler puts it. I have italicized that last phrase in order to stress that, as with the wardrobe analogy that I introduce later in this chapter, Butler is *not* suggesting that the subject is free to choose which gender she or he is going to enact. 'The script', if you like, is always already determined within this regulatory frame, and the subject has a limited number of 'costumes' from which to make a constrained choice of gender style.

The idea of performativity is introduced in the first chapter of *Gender Trouble* when Butler states that 'gender proves to be performative – that is, constituting the identity it is purported to be. In this sense, gender is always a doing, though not a doing by a subject who might be said to pre-exist the deed' (GT: 25). She then quotes the claim Nietzsche makes in *On the Genealogy of Morals* that 'there is no "being" behind doing, acting, becoming; "the doer" is merely a fiction imposed on the doing – the doing itself is everything' (1887: 29), before adding her own gendered corollary to his formulation: 'There is no gender identity behind the expressions of gender; that identity is performatively constituted by the very "expressions" that are said to be its results' (GT: 25).

This is a statement that has confused many people. How can there be a performance without a performer, an act without an actor? Actually, Butler is not claiming that gender is a performance, and she distinguishes between performance and performativity (although at times in *Gender Trouble* the two terms seem to slide into one another). In an interview given in 1993 she emphasizes the importance of this distinction, arguing that, whereas performance presupposes a pre-existing subject, performativity contests the very notion of the subject (GP: 33). In this interview Butler also explicitly connects her use of the concept 'performativity' to the speech act theory of J.L. Austin's *How To Do Things With Words* (1955) and Derrida's deconstruction of Austin's ideas in his essay 'Signature Event Context' (1972). Both of these texts will be discussed in detail in Chapter 4 when we look at Butler's theorizations of language, but here it should be noted that, although neither Austin nor Derrida is in evidence in *Gender Trouble*, Butler implicitly draws from their linguistic theories in her formulations of gender identity.

How is linguistic performativity connected to gender? Towards the beginning of *Gender Trouble* Butler states that '[w]ithin the inherited discourse of the metaphysics of substance, gender proves to be performative, that is, constituting the identity it is purported to be' (GT: 24–5). Gender is an act that brings into being what it names: in this context, a 'masculine' man or a 'feminine' woman. Gender identities are constructed and constituted by language, which means that there is no gender identity that precedes language. If you like, it is not that an identity 'does' discourse or language, but the other way around – language and discourse 'do' gender. There is no 'I' outside language since identity is a signifying practice, and culturally intelligible subjects are the effects rather than the causes of discourses that conceal their workings (GT: 145). It is in this sense that gender identity is performative.

At this point, we might return to the wardrobe analogy I explored earlier (see p. 50), where I argued that one's gender is performatively constituted in the same way that one's choice of clothes is curtailed, perhaps even predetermined, by the society, context, economy, etc. within which one is situated. Readers familiar with Daphne du Maurier's novel *Rebecca* (1938) will remember that the nameless narrator shocks her husband by turning up at a party in an identical dress to that worn by his dead wife on a similar occasion. In preparation for the party, the narrator, assisted by the malign Mrs Danvers, believes that she is choosing her costume and thereby creating herself, whereas it turns out that Mrs Danvers is in fact recreating the narrator as Rebecca. If Mrs Danvers is taken to exemplify authority or power here, *Rebecca* may provide an example of the way in which identities, far from being chosen by an individual agent, precede and constitute those 'agents' or subjects (just as Rebecca literally precedes the narrator).

SURFACE/DEPTH

Butler's argument that there is no identity outside language leads her to reject the commonly-accepted distinction between surface and depth, the Cartesian dualism between body and soul. In the third chapter of *Gender Trouble* she draws from Foucault's book *Discipline and Punish*, in which he challenges 'the doctrine of internalization', the theory that subjects are formed by internalizing disciplinary structures. Foucault replaces this with 'the model of inscription': as Butler describes it, this is the idea that '[the] law is not literally internalized, but incorporated, with the consequence that bodies are produced which signify that law on and through the body' (GT: 134–5). Because there is no 'interior' to gender 'the law' cannot be internalized, but is written on the body in what Butler calls 'the corporeal stylization of gender, the fantasied [*sic*] and fantastic figuration of the body' (GT: 135). Butler repeatedly refutes the idea of a pre-linguistic inner core or essence by claiming that gender acts are not performed by the subject, but they performatively constitute a subject that is the effect of discourse rather than the cause of it: '*That the gendered body is performative suggests that it has no ontological status apart from the various acts which constitute its reality*', she writes (GT: 136; my emphasis). Once again we return to the notion that there is no doer behind the deed, no volitional agent that knowingly 'does' its gender, since the gendered body is inseparable from the acts that constitute it. All the same, in the account of parody and drag that follows this description it does at times sound as though there *is* an actor or a 'doer' behind the deed, and Butler later admits that in *Gender Trouble* she 'waffled' between describing gender in terms of linguistic performativity and characterizing it as straightforward theatre. Her theories are clarified in *Bodies That Matter* where Butler emphasizes the Derridean and Austinian underpinnings of performativity that are as yet only implicit in *Gender Trouble*.

PARODY AND DRAG

'If the inner truth of gender is a fabrication and if a true gender is a fantasy instituted and inscribed on the surface of bodies, then it seems that genders can be neither true nor false, but are only produced as the truth effects of a discourse of primary and stable identity', Butler writes in the third chapter of *Gender Trouble* (GT: 136). In that case, it must be possible to 'act' that gender in ways which will draw attention to the constructedness of heterosexual identities that may have a vested interest in presenting themselves as 'essential' and 'natural', so that it would be true to say that all gender is a form of parody, but that some gender performances are more parodic than others. Indeed, by highlighting the disjunction between the body of the performer and the gender that is being performed, parodic performances such as drag effectively reveal the imitative nature of *all* gender identities. '*In imitating gender, drag implicitly reveals the imitative structure of gender itself – as well as its contingency*', Butler claims; 'part of the pleasure, the giddiness of the performance is in the recognition of a radical contingency in the relation between sex and gender' (GT: 137–8; her emphasis).

Gender is a 'corporeal style', an act (or a sequence of acts), a 'strategy' which has cultural survival as its end, since those who do not 'do' their gender correctly are punished by society (GT: 139–40); it is a repetition, a copy of a copy and, crucially, the gender parody Butler describes does not presuppose the existence of an original, since it is the very notion of an original that is being parodied (GT: 138). Gender performatives that do not try to conceal their genealogy, indeed, that go out of their way to accentuate it, displace heterocentric assumptions by revealing that heterosexual identities are as constructed and 'unoriginal' as the imitations of them.

Gender does not happen once and for all when we are born, but is a sequence of repeated acts that harden into the appearance of something that's been there all along. If gender is 'a regulated process of repetition' taking place in language, then it will be possible to repeat one's gender differently, as drag artists do (and you might also recall my wardrobe analogy – the ripped clothes and the sequins representing my attempts to 'do' my gender in subversive and unexpected ways). As I argued previously, you cannot go out and acquire a whole new gender wardrobe for yourself, since, as Butler puts it, '[t]here is only a taking up of the tools where they lie, where the very "taking up" is enabled by the tool lying there' (GT: 145). So you have to make do with the 'tools', or in my example, the 'clothes' that you already have, radically modifying them in ways which will reveal the 'unnatural' nature of gender.

There are two problems with this formulation: one is that the *manner* of taking up the tool will be determined as well as enabled by the tool itself – in other words, subversion and agency are conditioned, if not determined, by discourses that cannot be evaded. This leads to the second problem, which is that, if subversion itself is conditioned and constrained by discourse, then how can we tell that it is subversion at all? What is the difference between subversive parody and the sort of 'ordinary' parody that Butler claims everyone is unwittingly engaged in anyway? All gender is parodic, but Butler warns that '[p]arody by itself is not subversive' and she poses the important question as to which performances effect the various destabilizations of gender and sex she describes, and where those performances take place (GT: 139). There are some forms of drag that are definitely *not* subversive, but serve only to reinforce existing heterosexual power structures – in *Bodies*, Butler cites Dustin Hoffman's performance in *Tootsie* as an example of what she calls 'high het entertainment' (see Chapter 3, this volume), and we might also add the more recent film *Mrs Doubtfire* in which Robin Williams gives a cross-dressed performance as a nanny. Neither of these drag performances are subversive, since they serve to reinforce existing distinctions between 'male' and 'female', 'masculine' and 'feminine', 'gay' and 'straight'.

The question as to what constitutes 'subversive' as opposed to ordinary everyday gender parody, is not satisfactorily answered in the conclusion to *Gender Trouble*, 'From Parody to Politics', where Butler asserts that it *is* possible to disrupt what are taken to be the foundations of gender, anticipating *what* such parodic repetitions will achieve, without suggesting exactly *how* this can take place. Butler's claim on the penultimate page of *Gender Trouble* that '[t]he task is not whether to repeat, but how to repeat, or, indeed to repeat and, through a radical proliferation of gender, *to displace* the very gender norms that enable the repetition itself' (GT: 148) presents a similar problem: she has already asserted that to describe identity as an effect is not to imply that identity is 'fatally determined' or 'fully artificial and arbitrary', and yet at times it sounds as though the subject she describes *is* in fact trapped within a discourse it has no power to evade or to alter. In which case, 'how to repeat' will already be determined in advance, and what looks like agency is merely yet another effect of the law disguised as something different.

All the same, this is certainly not a view Butler expresses, and she seems optimistic about the possibilities of denaturalizing, proliferating and unfixing identities in order to reveal the constructed nature of heterosexuality. A proliferation of identities will reveal the ontological possibilities that are currently restricted by foundationalist models of identity (i.e. those theories which assume that identity is simply *there* and fixed and final). This is not, then, 'the death of the subject', or if it is, it is the theoretical death of an old, fixed subject, and the birth of a new, constructed one characterized by subversive possibility and agency. 'Construction is not opposed to agency; it is the necessary scene of agency', Butler affirms (GT: 147; see also CF: 15), and this leads her to refute another assumption popular among critics who are hostile to so-called 'postmodern' formulations of identity: '[t]he deconstruction of identity is not the deconstruction of politics; rather, it establishes as political the very terms through which identity is articulated' (GT: 148). Identity is intrinsically political, while construction

and deconstruction (note that they are not antithetical) are the necessary – in fact the *only* – scenes of agency. Subversion must take place
from within existing discourse, since that is all there is.

However, a number of important questions remain. We have
already encountered a potential difficulty in the attempt to differentiate between subversive and ordinary parody, and we still have not
answered the question as to what or who exactly is 'doing' the par-
odying. Indeed, if there is no pre-discursive subject, is it possible to
talk in terms of parody and agency at all, since both might seem
to presuppose an 'I', a doer behind the deed? How helpful is the notion
of parodic gender anyway? Does it really reveal the lack of an original
that is being imitated, or does it merely draw attention to the facti-
tiousness of the drag artist? Some of these questions and criticisms are
dealt with in the next section.

THE TROUBLE WITH *GENDER TROUBLE*

The fact that Butler's description of gender identity has raised so many
questions is a testament to its force, and at least some of *Gender Trouble*'s
importance lies in the debates it has generated amongst philosophers,
feminists, sociologists and theorists of gender, sex and identity, who
continue to worry over the meaning of 'performativity', whether it
enables or forecloses agency, and whether Butler does indeed sound
the death knell of the subject. In a written exchange with Butler, which
took place in 1991 and was published in 1995 as *Feminist Contentions:
A Philosophical Exchange*, the political philosopher Seyla Benhabib asserts
that feminist appropriations of Nietzsche, which Benhabib dubs 'the
"death of the subject" thesis', can only lead to self-incoherence. If there
is no gender identity behind the expressions of gender, asks Benhabib,
then how can women change the 'expressions' (by which she apparently means 'acts') by which they are constituted? 'If we are no more
than the sum total of the gendered expressions we perform, is there
ever any chance to stop the performance for a while, to pull the curtain
down, and let it rise only if one can have a say in the production of
the play itself?' (Benhabib *et al*. 1995: 21). Butler claims that the Self
is a masquerading performer, writes Benhabib, and 'we are now asked
to believe that there is no self behind the mask. Given how fragile and
tenuous women's sense of selfhood is in many cases, how much of a

hit and miss affair their struggles for autonomy are, this reduction of female agency to "a doing without the doer" at best appears to me to be making a virtue out of necessity' (Benhabib *et al.* 1995: 22).

The claim that the subject is necessary, if only as a fiction, has been made by other theorists, who are also likely to collapse 'performativity' into 'performance'. Indeed, this elision leads Benhabib to assume that there is a subjective entity lurking behind 'the curtain' – a notion that we know Butler refutes. Butler replies to Benhabib's (sometimes literal) misreadings in her essay 'For a Careful Reading', which is also included in *Feminist Contentions*, where she corrects the reduction of performativity to theatrical performance.

Two sociologists, John Hood Williams and Wendy Cealy Harrison, also question Butler's assertion that there is no doer behind the deed, although their critique is based on a clearer understanding of performativity than Benhabib's. Although they think it is helpful to deconstruct the idea of the ontological status of gender, they wonder whether a new ontology is founded on the equally foundationalist conception of gender performativity (Hood Williams and Cealy Harrison 1998: 75, 88). Feminist critic Toril Moi similarly objects that Butler has instated 'power' as her 'god' (1999: 47), and this does indeed raise the question as to whether one essential subject (stable, coherently sexed and gendered) has merely been replaced by another (unstable, performative, contingent). Furthermore, we might consider the ways in which the characterization of power as proliferating and self-subverting draws attention away from its oppressive and violent nature, a point that is made by the feminist theorist Teresa de Lauretis in her book, *Technologies of Gender* (though not in relation to Butler) (1987: 18). We have also seen that Butler's theories of discursively constructed melancholic gender identities might imply that the subject she describes is, like the Lacanian subject, negatively characterized by lack, loss and its enthralment to a pervasive and unavoidable law.

Hood Williams and Cealy Harrison also question the theoretical wisdom of combining speech act theory and psychoanalytic theory, since they argue that there is nothing citational about psychoanalytic accounts of identity (1998: 90). They find the assertion that there is no 'I' behind discourse curious for a theorist who is so interested in psychoanalysis, as psychoanalysis is centrally concerned with the 'I' and the process of its constitution (Hood Williams and Cealy Harrison 1998: 83). Furthermore, they describe Butler's reading of Freud as 'idiosyncratic' (1998: 85), while the theorist Jay Prosser also questions the accuracy of Butler's analysis of Freud, particularly a mis-citation of a key passage from Freud's *The Ego and the Id*, the theory that the body is a fantasized surface and a projection of the ego. Prosser's book is an 'attempt to read individual corporeal experience back into theories of "the" body' (1998: 7), so for him the question as to whether the body is a phantasmatic surface or a pre-existing depth is crucial. Claiming that formulations of transgendered identity are central to queer studies (and the transgendered individual is indeed important for both Butler and Foucault), Prosser rejects the notion that gender is performative, pointing out that 'there are transgendered trajectories, in particular *transsexual* trajectories, that aspire to that which this scheme [i.e. performativity] devalues. Namely, there are transsexuals who seek very pointedly to be nonperformative, to be constative, quite simply, to *be*' (1998: 32).

Butler addresses some of these criticisms in the Preface to the 1999 anniversary edition of *Gender Trouble*, where she acknowledges that the first edition of the book contains certain omissions, in particular, transgender, intersexuality, '[r]acialized sexualities' and taboos against miscegenation. Butler also accepts that her explanation of performativity is insufficient, and she admits that sometimes she does not distinguish between linguistic and theatrical performativity which she now regards as related (GTII: xxvi, xxv).

Butler's next book, *Bodies That Matter*, continues in similar interrogative mode, answering some of the questions arising from *Gender Trouble* and posing new and equally 'troubling' ones about 'the matter' of the body, its signification and its 'citation' in discourse.

SUMMARY

Gender Trouble calls the category of the subject into question as Butler engages in a genealogical critique that analyzes the conditions of the subject's emergence within discourse. Butler deploys psychoanalytic, Foucauldian and feminist theories in her discussions of homosexuality and heterosexuality and their mutual construction within the law. Heterosexual identities are constructed in relation to their abjected homosexual 'Other', but melancholic heterosexuals are haunted by the trace of this 'Other' which is never finally or fully abjected. This means that identities are by no means as straight, straightforward or singular as they appear and may be subversively worked against the grain in order to reveal the unstable, resignifiable nature of *all* gender identities. Some of these subversive practices are outlined in *Gender Trouble* and are analyzed further in her next book, *Bodies That Matter*.

3

SEX

THE MATTER OF MATTER

Now that you've read *Gender Trouble*, you are fully convinced that gender is the effect rather than a cause of discourse; you are highly suspicious of the category of 'the subject', since you know that it is constructed on the basis of the violent exclusion of those 'Others' who in some way do not conform to the heterosexual matrix. Although you're concerned by the intrinsically oppositional nature of identity, you derive some comfort from the possibilities of agency and subversion that open up when Hegelian dialectic (the subject constructed through opposition) is supplemented with a Foucauldian model of power (power as multiple, dispersed, spawning resistance). Fully aware of the difference between performativity and performance, you are now setting your mind to devising ways in which your gender, which you know is a discursively constituted series of acts, could be re-enacted against the grain of the heterosexual matrix. Perhaps you are also thinking about your melancholic gender identity and wondering how you could 'do' your gender differently in order to signal the desires you've had to reject in order to constitute yourself as a stable subject. It might not be entirely practical for you to turn up at work in drag tomorrow, but you're sure there must be less dramatic performative acts that will effectively draw attention to gender's constituted and constructed nature.

So far so good, except perhaps for the disconcerting habit I seem to have adopted of addressing you directly. The realizations you've made are all very well in the context of gender, but what about the matter of the body? It's one thing to argue that gender is constructed, and it doesn't take much of an imaginative leap to agree with de Beauvoir that 'one is not born, but rather becomes, a woman', but surely both Butler and de Beauvoir would have to accept that 'woman'- (or indeed 'man'-) as-constructed does not include sex? Fair enough, people are not born 'masculine' or 'feminine', but these theorists must concede that one is born 'male' or 'female'? To assert otherwise would be to throw the metaphorical (or perhaps in this case the literal) baby out with the bathwater. In fact, hasn't anyone ever told Butler where babies come from? Or, as she puts it in the Preface to *Bodies That Matter*, couldn't someone simply take her aside? (BTM: x).

THE BODY AND DISCOURSE

Actually, Butler's assertion that bodies are discursively constructed should come as no surprise, since she has already dealt with the matter of 'matter' in her two articles on de Beauvoir, as well as in another early piece on Foucault ('Foucault and the Paradox of Bodily Inscriptions') and in *Gender Trouble*. In both of these works Butler rejects the distinction between sex and gender, and in *Gender Trouble* she even asserts that sex *is* gender. If we accept that the body cannot exist outside of gendered discourse, we must also concede that there is no body that is not always already gendered. This does not mean that there is no such thing as the material body, but that we can only apprehend that materiality through discourse. 'As a locus of cultural interpretations, the body is a material reality which has already been located and defined within a social context', Butler writes in her article 'Sex and Gender in Simone de Beauvoir's *Second Sex*', where she deploys an existentialist idiom. 'The body is also the situation of having to take up and interpret that set of received interpretations . . . "existing" one's body becomes a personal way of having to take up and interpret that set of received gender norms' (SG: 45).

'To exist' one's body is not quite the same as 'to be' it, since the former implies that we have a degree of agency and choice when it comes to the matter of matter. But how can that be? And how could it possibly be true that, as Butler asserts, gender is 'a modality of taking on or realizing possibilities, a process of interpreting the body, giving it cultural form'? (SG: 36). What does it mean to give the body a cultural form? Surely it already has one, and isn't it true that most of us are bound to accept the bodies we already have? Moreover, how do Butler's arguments apply in the context of 'race' and 'the raced' body?

Bodies That Matter is not a book about how to change your body by piercing it or inscribing it with tattoos or going on a weight loss/weight _____ _____ practices, although they might well alter _____ _____ _____ take place upon a 'site' _____ nstituted.

_____ ard in *Bodies* are develop- _____ *Trouble*, in particular, her _____ mativity and the material _____ led explanation in *Bodies*, _____ specifically links it to the _____ *ationality* will be dealt with in the sections that follow, as will Butler's theorizations of interpella- tion, signification and discourse. If *Gender Trouble* is a genealogical investigation into gender ontologies (see p. 48), then *Bodies* could be described as a genealogy of the discursive construction of bodies or, as Butler puts it, the book is 'a poststructuralist rewriting of discur- sive performativity as it operates in the materialization of sex' (BTM: 12). Throughout her analyses, Butler is careful to emphasize that sexu- ality and sex do not precede 'race', and she now adds 'race' to the equation of what contours the body (BTM: 18). We will see what happens when 'race', sex and sexuality are read through (or indeed, *as*) discourse, performativity and citationality.

THE BOOK

Many readers find *Gender Trouble* confusing, difficult and dense, and possibly still more are bewildered by *Bodies That Matter*. Like *Gender Trouble*, the book does not have a linear structure and does not progress 'logically' from one concept to another. There are no clearly- demarcated sections on key issues such as performativity, citationality, resignification, and the index contains only names. Moreover, Butler appears to be making a virtue of eclecticism: towards the beginning of the book she claims that she does not draw from so many 'diverse traditions of writing' in order to assert that a single heterosexual imperative runs through each or all of them, but she is aiming to show how the unstable sexed body constitutes a challenge to the boundaries of symbolic intelligibility (BTM: 16). Indeed, it is part of Butler's political project to seek out the limits of discursive intelligibility in *Bodies*, so that, as in *Gender Trouble*, she can draw attention to those identities and bodies that currently 'matter' and those that don't. Again, as in *Gender Trouble*, Butler will assert that sexed identities are taken on through the violent rejection and exclusion (or 'foreclosure') of identities that are deemed *not* to matter, i.e. not to count within a heterosexual matrix which has a vested interest in preserving its own stability and coherence at the expense of 'other' identities.

In her discussions of Jennie Livingston's film *Paris is Burning* (1990) and Nella Larsen's novella *Passing* (1929), Butler pays particular attention to what she calls 'the racialization of gender norms' (BTM: 182). Butler insists that sex, sexuality and gender do not precede 'race', although we will see that her own focus sometimes appears to endorse such a privileging by failing to integrate the matter of 'race' into her other analyses of subject-formation. Butler's most extended analyses of 'race' take place in the fourth and sixth chapters of *Bodies* following her more theoretical and abstract discussions of interpellation, signification and performativity. For this reason I will consider 'race' in a separate section towards the end of this chapter; not in order to endorse the privileging of gender, sex and sexuality, but because Butler's analyses of 'race' will make little sense outside the theoretical frameworks that precede their discussion in *Bodies*. So far I have been placing the word 'race' in inverted commas in order to indicate that it is a problematic, unstable and by no means self-evident term. Since it would be unwieldy to continue to do so, from now on I shall dispense with the quotation marks; however, you should note that the word is always accompanied by *invisible* quotation marks both here and elsewhere in this book.

As in previous chapters, it will not be possible to give detailed analyses of the wide range of philosophers from whom Butler draws, so in the sections that follow I will concentrate on the following issues: interpellation and the assumption of sex; signification; constructivism; performativity; the matter of race; (re)citation and subversion.

INTERPELLATION AND THE ASSUMPTION OF SEX

> Birth, and copulation, and death.
> That's all the facts when you come to brass tacks.
>
> (T.S. Eliot)

This statement is made by Sweeney, the protagonist in T.S. Eliot's unfinished play *Sweeney Agonistes*. It is a stark reduction of existence into three nouns or 'facts', as if birth and sex and death are the only events we can be certain of in our lives, and yet Butler calls even these into question. Her adoption of de Beauvoir's dictum that 'one is not born, but rather becomes, a woman' has already complicated 'birth', and her extended analysis of 'sex' in *Bodies That Matter* further casts Sweeney's 'brass tacks' into doubt. Death is not a subject Butler tackles in any great detail (see Prosser 1998: 55 and SI for Butler on death and discourse).

By 'sex' Butler is not referring to 'sexual intercourse', but to one's sexed identity. Whether you tick the 'male' or 'female' box on census forms or application forms usually depends on whether you possess recognizably male or female genitalia, and it is on this basis that your sexed identity is allocated to you when you are born. To talk in terms of the 'allocation' of sex is already to assume that it is not 'natural' or given, and in her brief description of the 'sexing' which takes place at the scene of birth, Butler relies on the notion of *interpellation*. She writes:

> Consider the medical interpellation which (the recent emergence of the sono-gram notwithstanding) shifts an infant from an 'it' to a 'she' or a 'he', and in that naming the girl is 'girled', brought into the domain of language and kinship through the interpellation of gender. But that 'girling' of the girl does not end there; on the contrary, that founding interpellation is reiterated by various authorities and throughout the various intervals of time to reinforce or contest this naturalized effect. The naming is at once the setting of a boundary, and also the repeated inculcation of a norm.
>
> (BTM: 7–8)

Whether it takes place before birth through an ultrasound scan, or when the infant is born, the interpellation of sex and gender occurs as soon as a person's sex is announced – 'It's a girl/boy!'. A dictionary definition of the verb 'to interpellate' will tell you that it is the action of appealing to someone, a summons, citation or interruption, but Butler uses 'interpellation' in a specifically theoretical sense to describe how subject positions are conferred and assumed through the action of 'hailing'. To adapt de Beauvoir's statement, cited earlier, we might say 'One is not born, but rather one is called, a woman'. Butler draws this idea from Althusser's essay, 'Ideology and Ideological State Apparatuses', where he uses the term interpellation to describe the 'hailing' of a person into her or his social and ideological position by an authority figure. Althusser gives the example of a policeman calling out 'Hey, you there!' to a man [*sic*] in the street. By calling out, the policeman interpellates the man as a subject, and by turning around the man takes up his position as such. 'By this mere one-hundred-and-eighty-degree physical conversion [i.e. turning around] he becomes a *subject*', Althusser writes. 'Why? Because he has recognized that the hail was "really" addressed to him, that "it was *really* him who was hailed" (and not someone else) . . . The existence of ideology and the hailing or interpellation of individuals as subjects are one and the same thing' (Althusser 1969: 163).

There are all sorts of ways in which people are interpellated by ideology and you don't need a policeman in the street to shout out 'Hey, you there!' in order to be constituted as a subject. In fact, a (relatively benign) example of interpellation occurred in the first paragraph of this chapter when I addressed you, the reader, directly, writing as if I knew you and what you have read and what you think about what you have read. In doing so I was interpellating you, both literally by addressing you (as I am doing now) and in an Althusserian sense by implicitly slotting you into a preconceived 'readerly' and theoretical role ('You have read *Gender Trouble* haven't you? And you understand it/agree with it don't you?'). In making these assumptions I am effectively constituting you as a subject – in this specific context, as a *reading* subject, who is not only familiar with *Gender Trouble* and all the arguments in it, but who also agrees with them. A literary example of interpellation occurs in Thomas Hardy's novel, *Tess of the d'Urbervilles* (1891), which is subtitled 'A Pure Woman'. In the novel, Angel Clare interpellates Tess as 'pure' in a moral sense by assuming that she is an innocent virgin who has no knowledge of men, and it could be argued that she in turn constructs herself according to his model of 'proper' femininity until this construction becomes unsustainable.

Crucially however, interpellation cannot be one-sided, and in order for it to be effective you have to recognize yourself as the subject who is 'hailed' by metaphorically turning around – Althusser's 'mere one-hundred-and-eighty-degree physical conversion'. If read literally, Butler's example of the infant who is sexed when she or he is proclaimed a girl or a boy either at or before birth does not work, because (as far as we know) a foetus or an infant does not 'turn around' and recognize itself when someone declares 'It's a girl/boy!' This objection is not just a quibble, since Butler makes much of the importance of recognition and the subject's response to the law in the chapter on interpellation in *The Psychic Life of Power* ('"Conscience Doth Make Subjects of Us All": Althusser's Subjection'). Butler's extended analysis of recognition and what she calls Althusser's 'doctrine of interpellation' will be dealt with in Chapter 5 of this book.

To theorize sex in terms of interpellation as Butler does is to imply that one's body parts (particularly penis and vagina) are not simply and naturally 'there' from birth onwards, but that one's sex is performatively constituted when one's body is categorized as either 'male' or 'female' (we will deal with the issue of performativity in a later section; see also Chapter 2). In the fourth chapter of *Bodies* ('Gender is Burning: Questions of Appropriation and Subversion') Butler spends some time considering how subject positions are assumed in response to what she calls the 'reprimand' of the law – i.e. the policeman's call. Unlike Althusser, who regards this hailing as 'a unilateral act', Butler argues that interpellation is not 'a simple performative', in other words, it does not always effectively enact what it names, and it is possible for the subject to respond to the law in ways that undermine it. Indeed, the law itself provides the conditions for its own subversion (BTM: 122).

Butler recognizes that acts of disobedience must always take place *within* the law using the terms that constitute us: we have to respond to the policeman's call otherwise we would have no subject status, but the subject status we necessarily embrace constitutes what Butler (borrowing from Gayatri Chakravorty Spivak) calls 'an enabling violation'. The subject or 'I' who opposes its construction draws from that construction and derives agency by being implicated in the very power structures it seeks to oppose. Subjects are always implicated in the relations of power but, since they are also enabled by them, they are not merely subordinated to the law (BTM: 122–3).

If one is 'hailed' into sex rather than simply born a 'woman', then it must be possible to take up one's sex in ways which undermine *heterosexual hegemony*, where hegemony refers to the power structures within which subjects are constituted through ideological, rather than physical, coercion (the term 'hegemony' was originated by the Italian Marxist philosopher, Antonio Gramsci, 1891–1937). A girl is not born a girl, but she is 'girled', to use Butler's coinage, at or before birth on the basis of whether she possesses a penis or a vagina. This is an arbitrary distinction, and Butler will argue that sexed body parts are *invested* with significance, so it would follow that infants could just as well be differentiated from each other on the basis of other parts – the size of their ear lobes, the colour of their eyes, the flexibility of their tongues. Far from being neutral, the perception and description of the body ('It's a girl!', etc.) is an interpellative performative statement, and the language that seems merely to describe the body actually constitutes it. Again, Butler is not refuting the 'existence' of matter, but she insists that matter can have no status outside a discourse that is always constitutive, always interpellative, always performative. We will return to the perceived body – what you could call a phenomenology of body parts – later when we consider Butler's discussions of the psychoanalyst, Lacan.

DISCOURSE AND SIGNIFICATION

The idea that sex is an effect rather than a cause, and a repeated effect at that, will be familiar to you from *Gender Trouble*, where Butler argues that gender is the effect rather than the cause of discourse, 'the repeated stylization of the body, a set of repeated acts within a highly rigid regulatory frame that congeal over time to produce the appearance of substance, of a natural sort of being' (GT: 33). In *Bodies* Butler deploys the same argument in order to reveal how the apparently 'natural' body turns out to be a 'naturalized effect' of discourse. This is *the body as signified and as signification*, a body that can only be known through language and discourse – in other words, a body that is linguistically and discursively constructed. It is for this reason that 'sex' is placed within inverted commas, in order to signal its status *as* signification and its vulnerability to *re*signification.

In the first chapter of *Bodies* Butler insists on what she calls 'the indissolubility of . . . materiality and signification' – the body is signified in language and has no status outside a language which *itself* is material – and she asks whether language can simply refer to materiality or whether it is the very condition for materiality? (BTM: 31). Butler returns to this question in the next chapter of *Bodies*, where she continues to emphasize the materiality of language and the linguistic nature of materiality: 'language and materiality are not opposed, for language both is and refers to that which is material, and what is material never fully escapes from the process by which it is signified' (BTM: 68; see also Moi 1999: 49).

The term 'materialization' encapsulates the idea that the body is a temporal process repeatedly taking place in language that is *itself* material (the body as a *situation* as she claims in the early article I quoted above). The body, as Butler puts it in her introduction to *Bodies*, is '*a process of materialization that stabilizes over time to produce the effect of boundary, fixity, and surface we call matter*' (BTM: 9; her emphasis). Like gender, sex stabilizes or 'congeals' into the appearance of a reality or a 'natural fact', but to accept the 'reality' of sex (which is no reality at all) would be to allow what Butler now calls heterosexual hegemony to go unchallenged. On the other hand, a genealogical analysis of sex will deconstruct the body in order to show how and what different body parts have come to signify and how and what they may come to *re*signify.

CONSTRUCTIVISM AND ITS DISCONTENTS

It might be tempting to label Butler a 'radical constructivist', a position that would hold simply (and perhaps doggedly) that everything is language, everything is discourse – in other words, everything, including the body, is *constructed*. However, Butler claims that this misses the point of a deconstructive approach, which is not reducible to the statement that 'everything is discursively constructed' (BTM: 6). To deconstruct is to acknowledge and to analyze the operations of exclusion, erasure, foreclosure and abjection in the discursive construction of the subject (BTM: 8). As in *Gender Trouble*, we find ourselves within a dialectical matrix, but now it is 'sex' which is allocated and assumed on the basis of opposition and violent exclusion. Again, as before, Butler will describe sexed identities in terms of their melancholic structures (the 'abjection' and 'disruptive return' in the phrase quoted above), by which she is referring to her idea that, in order to secure a coherent heterosexual identity, a primary homosexual desire must be overcome.

By problematizing perceptions of 'constructivism', Butler implicitly responds to a number of the criticisms that were made of *Gender Trouble*. To talk of gender or sex as a 'construction' may invite the question, 'Well, who or what is doing the constructing then?' Butler clears up this point by asserting that construction is not 'a unilateral process initiated by a prior subject'; nor are discourse and power single acts that can be personified or attributed to a single agent (in both *Bodies* and *The Psychic Life of Power* Butler criticizes Althusser for characterizing power in precisely this way). Crucially, Butler adopts Foucault's conceptualization of power as myriad, multiple and dispersed, a description we came across in *Gender Trouble*, asserting that 'it would be no more right to claim that the term "construction" belongs at the grammatical site of [the] subject, for construction is neither a subject nor its act, but a process of reiteration by which both "subjects" and "acts" come to appear at all. There is no power that acts, but only a reiterated acting that is power in its persistence and instability' (BTM: 9).

Foucault has been misconstrued as personifying power, but he does not describe power as a subject that 'acts', nor does he presuppose the existence of a doer behind the deed. In the phrase above 'reiterated acting' does not have a grammatical subject that precedes it so that we are left with a sequence of acts that congeal over time to produce the appearance of a stable, *powerful* agent. Sex is the effect of power, but there is no single agent wielding that power and power cannot be personified. As in *Gender Trouble*, we must stop looking for (or at) the 'doer' and focus instead upon 'the deed': in other words, we will be analyzing the *effects* rather than the causes of a power that is characterized as multiple, myriad and dispersed. It is in this sense that reductions of 'radical constructivism' miss the point, since they assume that there is someone doing the constructing, whereas by reversing cause and effect ('the subject wields power' vs. 'power wields the subject') Butler theorizes gender and sex as performative. Before we discuss performative sex, we will need to look at Butler's discussions of Foucauldian, Freudian and Lacanian bodies.

FREUD, LACAN AND THE LESBIAN PHALLUS

Towards the end of the second chapter of *Bodies*, 'The Lesbian Phallus and the Morphological Imaginary', Butler asserts that the lesbian phallus enacts the penis' vanishing, thereby opening up anatomical and sexual difference as sites of what she calls 'proliferative resignifications' (BTM: 89). Where do penises go when they vanish, and what exactly is a lesbian phallus anyway? Is it only lesbians who have them or does everyone possess one? If so, what should we do with them? And what or where is the morphological imaginary?

Let's start with the last question first and consider the terms of Butler's chapter title – 'morphological' and 'imaginary'; we will save the lesbian phallus for later, a deferral which might appeal to Butler, since the phallus is a displaced symbol (although she also claims that the phallus is 'always dissatisfying in some way', so it might be best not to get your hopes up) (BTM: 57). The dictionary definition of 'morphology' is 'the science of form', and in the psychoanalytic accounts under discussion, 'morphological' refers to the form assumed by the body in the course of ego formation. 'Imaginary' in this context does not simply mean 'imagination' or 'imagined', but is part of Lacan's three-fold distinction between *the imaginary, the symbolic and the real*:

- *the imaginary* is the realm of conscious and unconscious images and fantasies;
- *the symbolic order* refers to language, the system into which the infant is compelled to enter on leaving the imaginary; and
- *the real* is what lies outside the symbolic and the limits of speech.

Later in *Bodies* Butler calls the existence of 'the real' into question, and in the chapter under discussion she collapses Lacan's distinction between the symbolic and the imaginary (BTM: 79; see also CS). In what she calls a rewriting of the morphological imaginary, Butler now traces how and what certain body parts come to signify as the body acquires its bodily image and its morphology. As in *Gender Trouble*, Butler cites Freud's claim that 'the ego is first and foremost a bodily ego' (BTM: 59), but in *Bodies* she notes that Freud appears to vacillate between theorizing body parts as real or imagined. The Freudian subject comes to know its body through pain, and it would seem that for Freud there *is* in fact a body that precedes the ego's perception of it (Butler's reading of Freud on this point is contentious, and it has been disputed by Prosser (1998: 40–1)). 'Although Freud's language engages a causal temporality that has the body part precede its "idea", he nevertheless confirms the indissolubility of a body part and the phantasmatic partitioning that brings it into psychic experience', Butler claims (BTM: 59). In other words, a body part and the imagining of that body part (the 'phantasmatic partitioning' of the body) are insep-arable, so that the 'phenomenologically accessible body' (i.e. the body that is knowable by being perceived) and the material body are one and the same entity.

Lacan moves from Freud's body as known through experience (specifically, the experience of pain) to an analysis of the body as it is signified in language. Butler sees this as a 'rewriting' of Freud, whereby Lacan theorizes the morphology of the body as a psychically invested projection and idealization (BTM: 73). One's morphology or bodily form is fantasized by an ego that doesn't exactly precede the body since 'the ego *is* that projection [and] . . . it is invariably a bodily ego' (BTM: 73). In other words, the body and the ego cannot be theorized separately, since they are simultaneous projections of one another. Certain body parts are given significance in this fantasized body, and Butler uncovers the masculinism of Lacan's positioning of the phallus as the privileged bodily signifier, arguing that it is possible to appro-priate and recirculate the phallus so that it is no longer necessarily or intrinsically connected to the penis.

Butler focuses on two important essays by Lacan, 'The Mirror Stage as Formative of the Function of the I as Revealed in Psychoanalytic Experience' (1949) and 'The Signification of the Phallus' (1958). In 'The Mirror Stage', Lacan claims that an infant acquires a notion of its bodily integrity when it perceives its reflection in the mirror. Up until that point, the infant's bodily self-perception has been chaotic, scrambled, in pieces, what Lacan calls a 'homelette', but when it sees its reflection it gains a sense of its bodily contours and its physical differentiation from others. Butler argues that, in the Lacanian account of the body, it is not experiences such as pleasure and pain that consti-tute the body, but *language*. This is because the mirror stage coincides with the infant's entry into language or the symbolic order.

Language does not simply name a pre-existing body, but in the act of naming it constitutes the body; at this stage it would be useful to recall the definition of performativity as that aspect of discourse having the power to produce what it names, even though Butler is not specif-ically talking in terms of performativity here. She mentions 'the performativity of the phallus' only in passing ('briefly', as she herself acknowledges), but in her discussion of the lesbian phallus it becomes clear that both penis and phallus are retroactively constructed by, and in, discourse – in other words, they are performative.

Butler and Lacan part theoretical company over the issue of the phallus (although they largely seem to have been in agreement up until this point): whereas Lacan installs the phallus as a privileged signifier that confers meaning on other bodily signifiers, Butler regards the phallus as 'the effect of a signifying chain summarily suppressed' – in other words, it does not have a privileged or inaugural status on a signifying chain that does not make itself evident (BTM: 81). However, Lacan and Butler concur on one point: for both of them, penis and phallus are not synonymous, since the phallus is what Butler calls 'the phantasmatic rewriting of an organ or body part' (BTM: 81). More simply put, the phallus is the *symbol* of the penis, it is not the penis itself.

Butler and Lacan's theorizations of the phallus may be seen as a struggle between the two theorists over the signification and symbol-ization of both penis and phallus: whereas Lacan asserts the primacy of the phallic signifier, Butler topples the phallus from the privileged position Lacan gives it. The disconnection of phallus and penis is crucial for Butler, since, if the phallus is no more than a symbol, then it could just as well symbolize any other body part, and those who neither 'have' nor 'are' the phallus (an important distinction for both Butler and Lacan) may 'reterritorialize' this symbol in subversive ways (BTM: 86). The disjunction between signifier (phallus) and referent (penis) allows Butler to remove the phallus from an exclusively male domain and to collapse the distinction between 'being' and 'having': in fact, *no one* 'has' the phallus, since it is a symbol, and disconnecting phallus from penis means that it may be redeployed by those who don't have penises.

'BEING' AND 'HAVING' THE PHALLUS

According to Lacan, a defining moment in sexual development occurs when the infant perceives that its mother desires a phallus that she does not possess. 'The child wishes to be the phallus in order to satisfy that desire', writes Lacan, but whereas the little boy actually 'has' the phallus, the little girl must 'be' it for someone else (when she grows up this will include her male partner who desires her phallic body). For Lacan, this is what

differentiates the sexes: whereas 'having' the phallus seems fairly unprob-
lematic for the lucky little boy, Lacan asserts that 'being' the phallus
requires a sacrifice of femininity on the part of the girl: 'in order to be the
phallus, that is to say, the signifier of the desire of the Other . . . a woman
will reject an essential part of femininity, namely, all her attributes in the
masquerade. It is for that which she is not that she wishes to be desired
as well as loved' (Lacan 1958: 290).

'The question, of course, is why it is assumed that the phallus requires
that particular body part to symbolize, and why it could not operate
through symbolizing other body parts', writes Butler, and she argues
that the 'displaceability' of the phallus, its ability to symbolize body
parts or body-like things other than the penis is what makes the lesbian
phallus possible (BTM: 84). Women can both 'have' and 'be' the phallus, which means that they can suffer from penis envy and a castration
complex at the same time; moreover, since 'the anatomical part is never
commensurable with the phallus itself', men may be driven by both
castration anxiety and penis envy, or rather, 'phallus envy' (BTM: 85).

The phallus is 'a transferable phantasm' (BTM: 86), 'an imaginary
effect' (BTM: 88), part of an imagined morphology (or a 'morphological imaginary') that can be appropriated and made to signify/
symbolize differently. Such 'aggressive reterritorializations' (BTM: 86)
deprivilege the phallus as both symbol and signifier, as well as revealing
its status within a bodily schema, which, like language, is a resignifiable signifying chain with no 'transcendental signified' at its origin.
Butler makes the most of this resignifiability in her ascription of
the phallus to other body parts: 'Consider that "having" the phallus
can be symbolized by an arm, a tongue, a hand (or two), a knee, a
pelvic bone, an array of purposefully instrumentalized body-like
things', she writes. '[T]he simultaneous acts of deprivileging the phallus
and removing it from the normative heterosexual form of exchange,
and recirculating and reprivileging it between women deploys the
phallus to break the signifying chain in which it conventionally operates' (BTM: 88).

Butler claims that the phallus is a 'plastic' signifier that may
'suddenly' be made to stand for any number of body parts, discursive
performatives or alternative fetishes (BTM: 89). And yet it would
appear that the phallus remains somewhat elusive, since Butler does

not specify exactly how such resignifications can 'suddenly' happen, or why women would *want* to make their arms, tongues, hands, pelvic bones, etc. into phallic signifiers. The subversive potential of the resignifiable phallus resides in Butler's insistence that you do not need to have a penis in order to have or be a phallus, and that having a penis does not mean that you will have or be a phallus. '[T]he lesbian phallus offers the occasion (a set of occasions) for the phallus to signify differently, and in so signifying, to resignify, unwittingly, its own masculinist and heterosexist privilege', she writes (BTM: 90).

Again we return to the idea that anatomy is discourse or signification rather than destiny, which means that the body can be resignified in ways that challenge rather than confirm heterosexual hegemony. In her conclusion to the second chapter of *Bodies*, Butler states that she is not suggesting that a new body part is required, since she has not been talking about the penis as such; instead she calls for the displacement of the symbolic heterosexual hegemony of sexual difference and the release of alternative imaginary schemas of erotogenic pleasure (BTM: 91). It would indeed appear that Butler has wrested this hitherto privileged signifier from Lacan's discursive control (BTM: 82–3), and yet the lesbian phallus she 'offers' in her description of alternative bodily schemas (BTM: 90) will be equally open to appropriation and resignification by those who do not identify as 'lesbians'. Indeed, we might well wonder who can 'have' and 'be' a lesbian phallus that is presumably vulnerable to subversive reterritorialization by men who, among other complexes, may also suffer from 'lesbian phallus envy'.

WIELDING THE LESBIAN PHALLUS

The lesbian phallus is not a dildo and it is not something one keeps in one's desk drawer (see GP: 37). The *morphological imaginary* is the morph or form the body takes on through imagined or fantasized projections, and Butler's rewriting of Lacan's morphological imaginary displaces the phallus from its privileged significatory position. Asserting that penis and phallus are not synonymous, Butler shows how the phallus may be 'reterritorialized' by people who do not have penises. This is because the phallus is a symbol of a body part whose absence or 'vanishing' it signifies. To disconnect sign (phallus) from referent (penis) in this way allows Butler to displace the privilege Lacan accords this phallic signifier. 'Of course there's also a joke in "The Lesbian Phallus" because to have the phallus in Lacan is also to control the signifier', Butler states in an interview. 'It is to write and to name, to authorize and to designate. So in some sense I'm wielding the lesbian phallus in offering my critique of the Lacanian framework. It's a certain model for lesbian authorship. It's parody' (GP: 37).

PERFORMATIVE BODIES

In the previous section we encountered Butler's glancing reference to the performativity of the phallus, and we have also looked in detail at her account of a discursively-constructed body which cannot be separated from the linguistic acts that name it and constitute it. Now we will turn to a statement Butler makes in the Introduction to *Bodies*, that, when it comes to the matter of bodies, the *constative claim is always to some degree performative* (BTM: 11). Remember the interpellative call of the policeman who hails the man in the street, or the doctor or nurse who exclaims 'It's a girl!' when the image of a foetus is seen on a scan. Now cast your mind back to Chapter 2 where I placed Butler's formulations of performative identities in the context of J.L. Austin's linguistic theories. In *Bodies That Matter* Butler once again draws from these lectures on linguistics, *How To Do Things With Words*. Austin distinguishes between two types of utterances, those that describe or report on something, and those that, in saying, actually perform what is being said. An example of the first, which Austin calls *constative utterances*, might be the statement, 'It's a sunny day', or 'I went shopping' (Austin also calls these *perlocutionary acts*); by saying 'I went shopping', I am not doing it, I am merely reporting an occurrence. On the other hand, if I am a heterosexual man standing in front of a registrar in a Register Office and I utter the words 'I do' in answer to the question, 'Do you take this woman to be your wife?', then I am actually performing the action by making the utterance: statements like these are called *performative utterances* or *illocutionary acts*. 'To name the ship *is* to say (in the appropriate circumstances) the words "I name &c." When I say, before the registrar or altar &c., "I do", I am not reporting on a marriage, I am indulging in it' (Austin 1955: 6).

To claim, as Butler does, that sex is always ('to some degree') performative is to claim that bodies are never merely described, they are always constituted in the act of description. When the doctor or nurse declares 'It's a girl/boy!', they are not simply reporting on what they see (this would be a constative utterance), they are actually assigning a sex and a gender to a body that can have no existence outside discourse. In other words, the statement 'It's a girl/boy!' is performative. Butler returns to the birth/ultrasound scene in the final chapter of *Bodies*, 'Critically Queer', where, as before, she argues that discourse precedes and constitutes the 'I', i.e. the subject:

> To the extent that the naming of the 'girl' is transitive, that is, initiates the process by which a certain 'girling' is compelled, the term or, rather, its symbolic power, governs the formation of a corporeally enacted femininity that never fully approximates the norm. This is a 'girl', however, who is compelled to 'cite' the norm in order to qualify and remain a viable subject. Femininity is thus not the product of a choice, but the forcible citation of a norm, one whose complex historicity is indissociable from relations of discipline, regulation, punishment.
>
> (BTM: 232)

'It's a girl!' is not a statement of fact but an interpellation that initiates the process of 'girling', a process based on perceived and *imposed* differences between men and women, differences that are far from 'natural'. To demonstrate the performative operations of interpellation, Butler cites a cartoon strip in which an infant is assigned its place in the sex–gender system with the exclamation 'It's a lesbian!'. 'Far from an essentialist joke, the queer appropriation of the performative mimes and exposes both the binding power of the heterosexualizing law *and its expropriability*', writes Butler (BTM: 232; her emphasis). We will return to expropriability and citation shortly; here the point to note is that, since sexual and gendered differences are performatively installed by and in discourse, it would be possible to designate or confer identity on the basis of an alternative set of discursively constituted attributes. Clearly, to announce that an infant is a lesbian is not a neutral act of description but a performative statement that interpellates the infant as such. 'It's a girl!' functions in exactly the same way: it is a performative utterance that henceforth compels the 'girl' to cite both sexual and gendered norms in order to qualify for subjecthood within the heterosexual matrix that 'hails' her.

'It is in terms of a norm that compels a certain "citation" in order for a viable subject to be produced that the notion of gender performativity calls to be rethought', Butler claims (BTM: 232). The term 'citation', highlighted in Butler's statement by its inverted commas, has been used throughout *Bodies* in a specifically Derridean sense that both differentiates it from, and aligns it with, performativity. The citation of sex and gender norms will be dealt with in the next section.

CITATIONAL SIGNS

In the previous section I quoted Butler's assertion that femininity is not a choice but the forcible citation of a norm. What exactly does it mean to cite sex or gender, and how does Butler use this term in *Bodies That Matter*? The *Oxford English Dictionary* definition of the verb 'to cite' reveals interesting etymological links with interpellation (although these are not connections Butler acknowledges). The word comes from the Latin *citare*, to set in motion or to call, and its meanings are listed as: 1) to summon officially to appear in a court of law; 2) to summon or arouse; 3) to quote; 4) to adduce proof; and 5) to call to mind, mention, refer to. The third, fourth and fifth dictionary definitions are closest to Butler's use of the term, but 'summoning' could also indicate the theoretical links between citation and interpellation.

Butler uses 'citation' in a specifically Derridean sense to describe the ways in which ontological norms are deployed in discourse, sometimes forcibly and sometimes not. Derrida's essay, 'Signature Event Context', is a response to Austin's claim that performative utterances are only 'successful' if they remain within the constraints of context and authorial intention. According to Austin, in order for a statement to have performative force (in other words, in order for it to enact what it names), it must 1) be uttered by the person designated to do so in an appropriate context; 2) adhere to certain conventions; and 3) take the intention(s) of the utterer into account. For example, if a brain surgeon stands at a church altar facing two people of the same sex and announces 'I pronounce you man and wife', the statement will have no performative force in the Austinian sense, since we can assume that the brain surgeon is not ordained and therefore is not the person authorized to marry the pair. Similarly, a priest who whispers 'I pronounce you man and wife' to his two teddy bears late at night before going to sleep is not conducting a marriage ceremony, even though he is authorized to do so, but is playing a game or having a fantasy. Clearly, *his* statement will have as little force as the unordained brain surgeon's, since 1) the context is inappropriate; 2) as with same-sex couples, in the UK and the US there is currently no law or convention regulating or permitting the marriage of toys; and 3) it is presumably not the priest's intention to marry his teddy bears to one another.

Austin spends some time attempting to distinguish felicitous from infelicitous performatives, and we will return to the distinctions he draws in Chapter 4 of this book. What is important at this stage is that Derrida seizes on the 'weakness' Austin discerns in the linguistic sign: after all, Austin would not attempt to differentiate between felicitous and infelicitous performatives if he did not know that statements are liable to be taken out of context and used in ways that their original utterers did not intend. Derrida asserts that what Austin regards as a pitfall or a weakness is in fact a feature of *all* linguistic signs that are vulnerable to appropriation, reiteration and, to return to the subject of this section, *re-citation*. This is what Derrida calls 'the essential iterability of [a] sign' which cannot be contained or enclosed by any context, convention or authorial intention (1972: 93). Rather, Derrida asserts that signs can be transplanted into unforeseen contexts and cited in unexpected ways, an appropriation and relocation that he calls citational grafting: all signs may be placed between quotation marks ('sex', 'race'), cited, grafted, and reiterated in ways that do not conform to their speaker's or writer's original intentions, and this means that, as Derrida puts it, the possibility of failure is intrinsic and necessary to the sign, indeed it is *constitutive* of the sign (1972: 97, 101–3).

These ideas will be familiar from *Gender Trouble* where, as I noted, Derrida is an implicit rather than a stated presence, and where failure, citation and re-citation are crucial to Butler's discussions of subversive gender performatives. In *Bodies*, Butler sees potential for subversion in Derrida's characterizations of the citational sign, and she now charts a move in her own theory from performativity to citationality, since rethinking performativity through citationality is deemed useful for radical democratic theory (BTM: 191; see also 14). Specifically, Butler asserts that Derrida's citationality will be useful as a queer strategy of converting the abjection and exclusion of non-sanctioned sexed and gendered identities into political agency.

In the final chapter of *Bodies*, Butler suggests that what she has called 'the contentious practices of "queerness"' exemplify the political enactment of performativity as citationality (BTM: 21). Butler is referring to subversive practices whereby gender performatives are 'cited', grafted onto other contexts, thereby revealing the citationality and the intrinsic – but necessary and *useful* – failure of all gender performatives. Butler gave examples of these practices in *Gender Trouble*, where she focused on parody and drag as strategies of subversion and agency. In *Bodies* she returns to drag as an example of what she calls 'queer trouble', and she finds other occasions for 'Nietzschean hopefulness' in the iterability and citationality of the sign. We will return to these ways of 'making trouble' in the next section but one.

THE MATTER OF RACE

Can race, like sex, sexuality and gender be cited and re-cited in ways that reveal the vulnerability of the terms of the law to appropriation and subversion? Is race an interpellated performative, and is a racial identity something that is 'assumed' rather than something one simply 'is'? Would it be possible once again to alter the terms of de Beauvoir's statement and affirm that 'one is not born but rather one becomes black/white'? Or could the word 'race' be substituted for 'sex' in Butler's description of *Bodies That Matter* as 'a poststructuralist rewriting of discursive performativity as it operates in the materialization of sex'? (BTM: 12).

Discussions of race were largely absent from *Gender Trouble*, and in *Bodies* Butler is careful to make the 'addition' of considerations of racial identity to her analyses of identity formation (BTM: 18). Accepting that normative heterosexuality is not the only regulatory regime operating in the production of the body, Butler asks what other 'regimes of regulatory production contour the materiality of bodies' (BTM: 17), and she asserts that '[t]he symbolic – that register of regulatory ideality – is also and always a racial industry, indeed, [it is] the reiterated practice of *racializing* interpellations' (BTM: 18; original emphasis). Butler rejects models of power that see racial differences as subordinate to sexual difference, and she argues that both racial and heterosexual imperatives are at work in reproductive and sexing practices.

Interpellations do not just 'call us' into sex, sexuality and gender, but they are also 'racializing' imperatives that institute racial difference as a condition of subjecthood. Sexual and racial differences are not autonomous or discrete axes of power (BTM: 116–17) and Butler repeatedly emphasizes that sex and gender are in no way prior to race. 'What appear within such an enumerative framework as separable categories are, rather, the conditions of articulation *for* each other', she states; 'How is race lived in the modality of sexuality? How is gender lived in the modality of race? How do colonial and neo-colonial nation-states rehearse gender relations in the consolidation of state power?' (BTM: 117).

These are the questions Butler sets herself, but in spite of this the 'matter' of race is not convincingly integrated into her discussions (which is why I am dealing with the question in a separate, penultimate section here). Although she analyzes how sex, sexuality and gender are interpellated, assumed and performatively constituted, there are no parallel discussions of performative race or *how* exactly race is interpellated by what Butler calls 'racializing norms'. Moreover, some critics might feel that it is important to preserve the distinction between the 'raced' body and the gendered/sexed/sexualized one. Remember the 'It's a lesbian!' joke: there the humour is derived from the fact that sexuality is not visible at birth, whereas by contrast race very often (although certainly not always) is. The African-American theorist Henry Louis Gates Jr effectively crystallizes this issue when he makes the following statement in his essay 'The Master's Pieces': 'it's important to remember that "race" is *only* a sociopolitical category, nothing more. At the same time – in terms of its practical performative force – that doesn't help me when I'm trying to get a taxi on the corner of 125th and Lenox Avenue. ("Please sir, it's only a metaphor.")' (1992: 37–8). Gates' wry observation shows that the visibly 'raced' body (black or white) cannot be theorized in exactly the same way as the sexualized, sexed or gendered body, although this is not to dispute Butler's assertion that all these vectors of power operate simultaneously and through one another.

It may be significant that Butler's most extended discussion of race centres on a novella by Nella Larsen, *Passing*, in which one of the protagonists attempts to 'pass' for white. Here the body is *not* visibly black, and Clare (the woman who is 'passing' for white) is only 'outed' (Butler's term, BTM: 170) when her white husband encounters her among a group of black people. Butler uses *Passing* to confirm her point that race and sexuality are imbricated and implicated, since she discerns an overlapping of the 'mute homosexuality' between the two women protagonists and Clare's 'muted' blackness, which, like homosexual desire, attempts to conceal itself (BTM: 175). Moreover, just as heterosexuality requires homosexuality in order to constitute its coherence, so 'whiteness' requires 'blackness' to offset itself and confirm its racial boundaries. Heterosexuality and whiteness are simultaneously destabilized in *Passing*, as queering – i.e. the desire between the two women – upsets and exposes both racial and sexual passing (BTM: 177). (For a discussion of race and melancholia, see Butler's interview 'On Speech, Race and Melancholia', 1999.) Butler's analysis of Larsen's novella similarly 'queers' psychoanalytic theory by exposing its assumption of the primacy of sexuality and whiteness. In fact, Butler sees *Passing* as a challenge to psychoanalytic theory, 'a theorization of desire, displacement, and jealous rage that has significant implications for rewriting psychoanalytic theory in ways that explicitly come to terms with race' (BTM: 182).

The other analysis of race in *Bodies* occurs in Butler's discussion of Jennie Livingston's *Paris is Burning*, (BTM: 121–40) a film about drag balls in Harlem that are attended by/performed by African-American or Latino/Latina 'men'. Again, Butler sees the film as exemplifying her assertion that sexual difference does not precede race or class in the constitution of the subject, so that the symbolic is also a racializing set of norms and the subject is produced by racially informed conceptions of 'sex' (BTM: 130). Butler's analyses of *Paris is Burning* and *Passing* lead her to conclude that the theoretical priority of homosexuality and gender must give way to a more complex mapping of power that places both terms in their specific racial and political contexts (BTM: 240).

Butler herself has been scrupulous in *not* suggesting that any one term takes priority over another, even though the organization of *Bodies* might suggest otherwise – if not the priority of sex over race, at least the separability of the terms. Since race is largely dealt with in discrete chapters (and, for that matter, these chapters are 'literary' rather than 'theoretical' in their focus), as I noted before, 'the matter', so to speak, remains somewhat at a distance from Butler's other theoretical discussions. We may be left with questions concerning the relationship between race and the lesbian phallus, or how Butler's description of 'girling' might be applied to race, since neither the lesbian phallus nor interpellation/performativity are specifically discussed in the context of race. All the same, to talk in terms of 'racializing norms' is indeed to suggest that race, like gender, sex and sexuality, is constructed rather than natural, assumed in response to the interpellative 'call' of discourse and the law, even though Butler is unspecific as to how exactly this 'call to race' takes place.

QUEER TROUBLE

In spite of the tragic outcome of both texts, Butler highlights the moments of promising instability in *Paris is Burning* and *Passing*. In Butler's analysis, *Paris is Burning* represents the resignification of normative heterosexual kinship (an issue to which Butler will return in *Antigone's Claim*), while *Passing* similarly reveals how hegemonic racial and sexual norms may be destabilized by subjects who do not fit neatly into the categories of white heterosexuality. Such norms are far from monolithic or stable, but, as we saw in a previous section, they may be reiterated and cited in ways that undermine heterosexual hegemony. (For an alternative reading of *Paris is Burning*, see bell hooks' essay, 'Is Paris Burning?' (1996).)

However, if all linguistic signs are citational, citationality in and of itself is not a subversive practice, and it follows that some signs will continue to work in the service of oppressive heterosexualizing norms (and this is something we already know from Butler's description of femininity as 'a *forcible* citation of the norm' (BTM: 232; my emphasis). Clearly, there are 'good' (subversive) citations and 'bad' (forced) citations, and the task will be to distinguish between them – which is not always easy as we shall see. Another problem is that discourse and the law operate by concealing their citationality and genealogy, presenting themselves as timeless and singular, while performativity similarly 'conceals or dissimulates the conventions of which it is a repetition' (BTM: 12). Again, it will be necessary to distinguish between those performatives which consolidate the heterosexual norm and those that work to reveal its contingency, instability and citationality.

In a previous example, I described an unordained brain surgeon who conducts a marriage ceremony that, in Austinian terms, will have no performative (or indeed legal) force because it falls outside recognized and sanctioned conventions. Butler, on the other hand, might assert that the utterance of 'I pronounce you, etc.' by someone who is not authorized to do so is a subversive political strategy, since it is a recitation of an unstable heterosexual norm that is always vulnerable to appropriation. There are alternative, equally subversive ways of citing heterosexual signs that are *all* vulnerable to appropriation: the lesbian phallus is one such 'recitation', and Butler gives other examples, some of which are theatrical. As in *Gender Trouble*, parody and drag are modes of queer performance that subversively 'allegorize' (to use Butler's term) heterosexual melancholy, thereby revealing the allegorical nature of *all* sexual identities. Although Butler is careful to distinguish performance from performativity in *Bodies*, she also asserts that theatre provides crucial opportunities for queer politics. '[A]n important set of histories might be told in which the increasing politicization *of* theatricality for queers is at stake', she writes. 'Such a history might include traditions of cross-dressing, drag balls, street walking, butch–femme spectacles . . . kiss-ins by Queer Nation; drag performance benefits for AIDS' (BTM: 233).

What Butler calls 'the increasing theatricalization of political rage in response to the killing inattention of public policy-makers on the issue of AIDS' is epitomized by the appropriation of the term 'queer', an interpellative performative that has been converted from an insult into a linguistic sign of affirmation and resistance (BTM: 233). And yet, although she continues to find subversive potential in the contingency and resignifiability of the sign, Butler is also aware that citation is not necessarily subversive and she points out that certain 'denaturalizations' of the heterosexual norm actually enforce heterosexual hegemony (BTM: 231). Such parodies may certainly be 'domesticated' so that they lose their subversive potential and function merely as what Butler calls 'high het entertainment', and Butler cites Julie Andrews in *Victor, Victoria*, Dustin Hoffmann in *Tootsie* or Jack Lemmon in *Some Like It Hot* as examples of drag performances that have been produced by the heterosexual entertainment industry for itself (further examples might include Julian Clary and Eddie Izzard) (BTM: 126). Such performances only confirm the boundaries between 'straight' and 'not straight' identities, providing what Butler calls 'a ritualistic release for a heterosexual economy that must constantly police its own boundaries against the invasion of queerness' (BTM: 126).

As before, it is difficult to disentangle subversive citations and performatives from the power structures they oppose, since subversion is necessarily and inevitably implicated in discourse and the law. However, this constitutes the promise as well as the problematic of performativity, and Butler argues that making use of existing 'resources' for subversive ends will require vigilance and hard work. 'How will we know the difference between the power we promote and the power we oppose?', she writes. The problem, of course, is that one *can't* know this in advance, so that subversive recitation will always involve a certain amount of risk. It is a risk that Butler well understands, as she once again submits her work to the scrutiny of readers who are likely to interpret and deploy her ideas in unforeseen ways. The effects of one's words are incalculable, since performatives and their significations do not begin or end (BTM: 241). Perhaps it will be appropriate to end with a 'citation' of Butler's concluding acknowledgement of the vulnerability of her own terms to appropriation and redeployment:

> It is one of the ambivalent implications of the decentering of the subject to have one's writing be the site of a necessary and inevitable expropriation. But this yielding of ownership over what one writes has an important set of political corollaries, for the taking up, reforming, deforming of one's words does open up a difficult future terrain of community, one in which the hope of ever fully recognizing oneself in the terms by which one signifies is sure to be disappointed. This not owning of one's words is there from the start, however, since speaking is always in some ways the speaking of a stranger through and as oneself, the melancholic reiteration of a language that one never chose, that one does not find as an instrument to be used, but that one is, as it were, used by, expropriated in, as the unstable and continuing condition of the 'one' and the 'we', the ambivalent condition of the power that binds.
>
> (BTM: 241–2)

This statement could be interpreted as a gesture of humility or a disclaimer of responsibility on Butler's part, and there may be contexts in which it is problematic to claim that one does not use language but is, rather, used by it. ('I didn't write those words! They wrote me.') Butler returns to the issues of speech acts, linguistic responsibility and the 'reach of . . . signifiability' (BTM: 241) when she analyzes hate speech, 'obscenity' and censorship in her next book, *Excitable Speech*.

SUMMARY

Bodies That Matter is a genealogy of the discursive construction of bodies. As in *Gender Trouble*, Butler describes how sexed identities, far from being stable, physical 'facts' of existence, are taken on and assumed through the violent foreclosure of identities that are deemed not to 'matter' within a heterosexual hegemony. Butler draws from a wide range of thinkers and writers to describe sex as interpellation (Althusser), performative (Austin), signification (Freud, Lacan), constructed (Foucault), and recitable (Derrida). The Austinian and Derridean underpinnings of her theories are made more explicit than in *Gender Trouble* as Butler now rethinks performativity through citationality, leading her to argue that, if sex is performative, the result of interpellation and citation, it may be recited in ways that destabilize heterosexual hegemony.

An example of such expropriation is the lesbian phallus, as what is only the *symbol* of a body part (penis) may be appropriated and recirculated by people who do not have penises. Butler is careful to consider how gender, sexual difference and race are connected vectors of power that in no way precede each other. 'Sexing practices' secure a heterosexual imperative, but they also consolidate (as well as contest) the boundaries of racial distinction. Butler gives examples of how racial, sexual and gender norms may be subverted, and yet she acknowledges that it is sometimes difficult to tell what is subversive and what merely consolidates existing power structures.

4

LANGUAGE

ISSUES

If there is no doer behind the deed as Butler asserts, then who or what should we prosecute or blame in cases of hate speech and 'obscenity'? (As we shall see, 'obscenity' is not a self-evident category.) Do words possess the power to wound and what legal instrument should deal with such 'injuries'? If power is productive rather than prohibitive as Foucault claims, society's censors may be implicated in generating and proliferating the discourses and representations they set out to ban. And if signs are unstable, reiterable and never finally determined by context or convention, it might be possible to resignify and recontextualize representations and words that are deemed to be wounding. In that case, perhaps it would be better to acknowledge and exploit the fact that no word or representation *inevitably* and always has the power to wound, rather than seeking recourse to a law that is itself by no means neutral or objective.

In *Excitable Speech* (1997) Butler enters the censorship debate as she places her continuing interrogation of subject-categories in the context of language, specifically hate-speech, gay self-expression and so-called pornographic and obscene representations. Butler analyzes the performativity of language (Austin), the efficacy of interpellation (Althusser) and the logic of prosecuting speakers who are not the sovereign agents of what they say (Foucault). As Butler explains, 'excitable speech' is a legal term referring to statements deemed to be beyond the utterer's control because they have been made under duress, and she argues that *all* speech is in some sense beyond the speaker's control (ES: 15). If all speech is excitable, then it would be possible for speakers to plead diminished responsibility when called to account for language that precedes and exceeds them: indeed, they might even say that they did not speak language but it spoke them (and Butler herself appears to state this at the end of *Bodies*). This is not a view Butler endorses, and it is an issue to which we will return. Throughout her analyses Butler insists that, although language is performative, it is not always 'felicitously' so ('felicitous' is Austin's term for statements that successfully enact what they name). Rather, failure will once again prove to be a crucial lever in Butler's account of the radical resignifiability of the sign.

WORDS THAT WOUND, WORDS THAT BIND

Some readers might assume that the distinction between utterance and action is self-evident: clearly, to talk about having sex or to represent it is not the same as actually doing it, and yet in the previous chapter we encountered Austin's theory that there are certain utterances that do indeed enact what they name. Austin contrasts *performative utterances* such as 'I name this ship . . .' with *constative statements* such as 'I went swimming', which are merely descriptive: to say you swam the Channel is not the same as doing it, whereas, in the correct context, the first statement ('I name this ship . . .') actually performs the deed in uttering it. In *Gender Trouble* and *Bodies*, Austin's distinction between performative and constative utterances is crucial to Butler's formulations of gender and sex as performative, although in both books Butler maximizes Austin's inability to distinguish clearly between performative and constative utterances. Indeed, Austin himself acknowledges that all utterance is in some sense an act, and that by saying something we are *always* doing something (1995: 92, 94).

If we accept the view that all utterance is action, then it would follow that calling someone 'nigger' or 'fag' is doing something, i.e. insulting them, so that there is only a difference of degree rather than kind between such verbal abuse and, for example, hitting someone or throwing a brick through their window. On the other hand, Austin attempts to distinguish between utterances that *actually* do something (sentencing someone to life imprisonment, pronouncing a heterosexual couple man and wife, naming a ship) and those that lead to certain consequences: he calls the former *illocutionary speech acts* while the latter are *perlocutionary speech acts*. Austin makes two important claims about the former: first, illocutionary acts are defined by their effects, what Austin calls 'uptake', and second, those effects come about as a result of the force of context and convention. Remember that, in Chapter 3, I gave the example of a priest who, in pronouncing his teddy bears man and wife before he goes to bed at night is not performing a performative or an illocutionary speech act. This is because there is no convention permitting the marriage of teddies, so that, even though the priest is authorized to perform marriages, his words will have no binding force when uttered in the privacy of his bedroom. On the other hand, if a heterosexual couple stand in front of an authorized person (a registrar, a priest) in an authorized place (a Register Office, a church), then the same words 'I pronounce you man and wife' will be legally binding and an illocutionary speech act will have taken place in which what is said has simultaneously been done.

In *How To Do Things With Words* Austin specifies naming a ship as a performative action, but he claims that the appropriate contexts and conventions must be in place if the statement is to be effective. 'To name the ship *is* to say (*in the appropriate circumstances*) the words "I name &c." When I say, before the registrar or altar &c., "I do", I am not reporting on a marriage, I am indulging in it' (Austin 1955: 6; my emphasis). The phrase 'in the appropriate circumstances' is crucial here, since if the circumstances are *not* appropriate the utterance will fail to achieve its desired effect. In another ship-naming example Austin hypothesizes that he might see a ship that is about to be named, walk up to it and smash a bottle against its side, proclaiming 'I name this ship *Mr Stalin*'. '[B]ut the trouble is I was not the person chosen to name it', Austin writes, which means that the ship in question will not be named *Mr Stalin*: 'it is a mockery', Austin says, 'like a marriage with a monkey [or perhaps a teddy bear]' (1955: 23–4). If I am not authorized to name a ship or to enact any other kind of performative, my utterances will fail. Saints cannot baptize penguins (another of Austin's examples), humans cannot marry monkeys, and Austin cannot name a ship *Mr Stalin* unless he has been authorized to do so. For Austin then, the outcome of a performative statement depends on convention and ritual.

However, Butler has already departed from this view of the sign in *Bodies That Matter*, and she does so again in *Excitable Speech*.

If we accept Austin's distinction between illocutionary and perlocutionary speech acts, then clearly it would be possible to argue, that in certain circumstances, actions could be construed as illocutionary speech acts that perform what they name in the act of uttering. However, in the introduction to *Excitable Speech*, Butler makes the following points to counteract Austin's view of language: first, as we saw in the previous chapter, words are not context- or convention-bound or, as Derrida would put it, the meaning of words is never ultimately 'saturable'. A speech act does not take place in the isolated moment of its utterance, but is the 'condensation' of past, present, and even future unforeseen meanings. It is in this sense that speech acts are 'excitable', or beyond their speakers' control (or even comprehension), and this means that, as Butler puts it, an utterance may always '[exceed] the moment it occasions' (ES: 14).

This leads to the second point, which is that, if language is a signifying chain stretching behind and beyond the utterer, then it would be a mistake to assume that the utterer is the sole originator of her or his speech. Butler rejects the notion of sovereign autonomy in speech, but, although she insists that speakers are never fully in control of what they say, she also argues that speakers are to some extent responsible for their utterances and in certain cases should be prosecuted for uttering words that wound. Sovereignty and responsibility are not synonymous, and speakers are formed by language as much as they form it. Butler therefore regards the question of responsibility as one that is 'afflicted with impurity from the start', while the paradox of non-sovereign speakers 'intimates an ethical dilemma brewing at the inception of speech' (ES: 28).

To posit a sole originator of an utterance is, as we shall see below, a fiction fabricated by the law in order to justify the regulation of speech and representation, and the 'ethical dilemma' Butler identifies concerns the question of who is culpable in the absence of a sovereign speaking subject. Butler also departs from Austin's connection of speaker and speech, speech and conduct: words do not always enact what they name and performatives are not necessarily effective or 'felicitous' – in other words, speech and act are not synonymous. Again, this is because neither context nor convention is binding, and no word will *inevitably* lead to a single, foregone conclusion. What Butler calls 'the open temporality of the speech act' contains the possibility for agency and resignification (or 'resigni-fication' as she writes it in *Excitable Speech*, the break introduced into the word presumably intended to signal similar 'breaks' that may be made with context and convention) (ES: 41). '[T]he gap that separates the speech act from its future effects . . . begins a theory of linguistic agency that provides an alternative to the relentless search for legal remedy', she writes. 'The interval between instances of utterance not only makes the repetition and resignification of the utterance possible, but shows how words might, through time, become disjointed by their power to injure and recontextualized in more affirmative modes' (ES: 15).

As in *Gender Trouble* and *Bodies*, repetition and resignification contain the promise of affirmative recontextualizations and subversive redeployments that constitute a more effective response to hate speech than legal measures. Perhaps it is just as well that Butler seeks alternatives to legal redress, since, as we shall see, she finds the law troublingly inconsistent in its arbitration of cases of race hate and sexual self-expression.

THE LAW

Both in *Excitable Speech* and in 'The Force of Fantasy', an article published seven years previously on the late photographer Robert Mapplethorpe and the right-wing former US Senator Jesse Helms, Butler argues that the law is libidinally invested in what it legislates (a literary example of this might be provided by Angelo in Shakespeare's *Measure for Measure*). In both texts she also claims that hate speech is recirculated by the authorities (i.e. senators, lawyers) who are supposed to regulate it, and since state speech is effectively synonymous with hate speech there will be little point seeking recourse to the law. As an example of the way the law co-opts the language that it seeks to adjudicate, Butler gives a close textual analysis of the legal discourse deployed in a court case concerning whether a burning cross placed on the front lawn of a black family constituted an act of race hate or an act of speech (ES: 52–65).

Before we consider what does and does not constitute speech, I want to elaborate on the productive, proliferative nature of the law, which, as we have seen, deploys the hate speech it is supposed to legislate. If the law produces hate speech in order to legislate it, it also produces a culpable speaking subject in order to prosecute him or her. The legal fabrication of the culpable speaking subject brings us back to the Nietzschean formulation that there is no doer behind the deed deployed in *Gender Trouble* and *Bodies That Matter*. In *Excitable Speech*, Butler once again quotes Nietzsche's assertion that 'there is no "being" behind doing, acting, becoming; "the doer" is merely a fiction imposed on the doing – the doing itself is everything' (1887: 29). In *Gender Trouble* Butler added a gendered corollary to this formulation: 'There is no gender identity behind the expressions of gender; . . . identity is performatively constituted by the very "expressions" that are said to be its results' (GT: 25), and *Excitable Speech* expands this idea to include all speech acts. We might substitute the terms of her sentence in the following way: 'there is no hate-speaker behind the expressions of hate speech; the identity of the hate-speaker is performatively constituted by the very "expressions" that are said to be its results'.

What are the implications of claiming that there is no hate-speaker behind the expressions of hate speech? Is this not rather a dangerous idea that could give racists/homophobes/misogynists the licence to go around insulting people and blaming 'discourse' for their actions? In fact, the suggestion that there is no hate-speaker behind the expressions of hate speech dovetails with Butler's idea that there are no sovereign agents of language and that language is a citational chain preceding and exceeding speaking subjects who are retroactively installed by and in discourse. This implies that speakers cannot be held ultimately responsible for utterances of which they are not the sole originators, so that to claim that there is no culpable subject behind the expressions of hate speech will require that we reconsider the efficacy of legal measures in such cases. If there is no doer behind the deed, then who are these people and of what do they stand accused? If they are not the sovereign agents of their hateful speech why are they being prosecuted? Why not prosecute discourse, or the ideology that interpellates speakers to behave in such a hateful way?

Clearly, it would not be practical or possible to prosecute discourse/ideology, and according to Butler it is for this reason that the law attributes agency to a sovereign subject that it fabricates in order to prosecute it. In a further glossing of Nietzsche's formulation, Butler asserts that a culpable subject is installed as prior to the deed in order to blame it and hold it accountable (ES: 45). Although the subject is *not* the intentional originator of its deed, this does not prevent the law from prosecuting a subject which is a pre-eminently *fictional* construct. By producing an accountable originator of injurious speech, the law sets up what Butler calls a 'moral causality' between the subject and its act, whereby, as she puts it, 'both terms [i.e. subject and act] are separated off from a more temporally expansive "doing" that appears to be prior and oblivious to these moral requirements' (ES: 45–6). The 'more expansive "doing"' Butler mentions here would presumably acknowledge that, since utterances take place on a citational chain whose historicity (to use her term) exceeds the subject, subjects are not uniquely accountable for their speech. Butler breaks the moral causality between subject and act that is taken for granted by the law, arguing instead that the subject is a 'belated metalepsis' and a subject-*effect* (ES: 50). A metalepsis is a substitution, and the subject-effect is 'belated' in the sense that it has been retroactively installed by the law at the scene of the crime, as it were. Put very simply, the law requires someone or something to blame in cases of hate speech and 'obscenity', so it points the finger at a subject that *it creates* in order to prosecute.

'Does tracing the injury to the act of a subject and privileging the juridical domain as the site to negotiate social injury not unwittingly stall the analysis of how precisely discourse produces injury by taking the subject and its spoken deed as the proper place of departure?', Butler asks (ES: 47). Although the genealogical analysis of discourse may well have been 'stalled' by anti-pornography campaigners such as Catharine MacKinnon and Mari Matsuda who focus on injury rather than on the operations of discourse, *Excitable* analyzes the discursive production of injury and the installation of the subject-effect. Indeed, Butler's discussions will make it more difficult to point the finger of blame, since it is no longer clear who or what is culpable in cases of hate speech or 'obscenity'.

INTERPELLATION REVISITED

Before considering the legal treatment of race hate and 'obscenity', we will need to take a brief detour via Althusser whose theorizations of interpellation and subject-constitution are once again crucial to Butler in *Excitable Speech*. You will remember from the previous chapter that Althusser's 'man in the street' is hailed by a policeman who calls out 'Hey, you there!' The man turns around, and in recognizing that the policeman is calling him, assumes his position as a subject, or to use Foucault's term, he is 'subjectivated'. Some readers may have been wondering how Butler manages to reconcile Althusser with Foucault, theoretically speaking. If power is multiple, myriad and dispersed, then why is the subject hailed by a single policeman on the street who is apparently the sovereign representative of the law? Moreover, if interpellation is a performative utterance, i.e. it constitutes the subject in the act of naming her or him, and if, as we know, utterances do not originate from a single sovereign utterer who is solely responsible for them, then why does the policeman's call appear to be so effective? Why does the man in the street turn around when the policeman calls out to him, and what would happen if he heard the call, ignored it and simply carried on walking?

In the introduction to *Excitable Speech* Butler revisits the Althusserian scene in a brief but important section on the injurious action of names. Noting that we require the names by which we are called in order to be constituted as subjects, Butler turns her attention to how name-calling operates. Although Althusser seems to ascribe divine and sovereign power to the policeman who hails the man in the street, Butler insists that there is no magical efficacy in the interpellative call of the law. Rather, interpellation is a citational utterance that relies on context and convention in order to be effective, which means that it is no different to other, similarly contingent utterances. 'In a sense, the police *cite* the convention of hailing', Butler argues, '[they] participate in an utterance that is indifferent to the one who speaks it' (ES: 33). Interpellation is therefore a citable, *ex*-citable utterance that exceeds the interpellator who is not in control of her or his speech.

Similarly, although Althusser posits a subject who turns around and reflexively appropriates the term when she or he is called, Butler asserts that the linguistic constitution of the subject may take place without the subject's even registering the operation of interpellation. So the law might call me and I might not hear, but the name by which I am called and of which I am ignorant will still constitute my social identity as a subject. On the other hand, I might refuse the name by which I am called, but according to Butler the name will nonetheless still continue to force itself upon me (ES: 33). So, although Butler notes the subject's 'readiness to be compelled' (an idea to which she returns in the fourth chapter of *The Psychic Life of Power*), subjects who do not willingly embrace the names they are called will nonetheless be constituted by them.

There is no reason that interpellative calls should be any more effective or binding than other performative utterances, and Butler finds potential for agency in the unstable nature of these performatives by placing Althusser's scene within a Foucauldian model of power and a Derridean linguistic framework. Once again drawing from Foucault's *The History of Sexuality Vol. I*, Butler asserts that power is not invested in a single divine subject, neither does it reside in a name, so that interpellation has no clear origin or end (ES: 34). If power cannot be localized or personified and if interpellative calls are not necessarily effective, then it will be possible to resignify linguistic terms that Butler claims have an open-ended semantic future. 'Interpellation', she claims, 'is an address that regularly misses its mark, it requires the recognition of an authority at the same time that it confers identity through successfully compelling that recognition' (although this 'compelling' of recognition is *not* always successful) (ES: 33). We cannot choose the terms by which we are interpellated, and, although it seems that we cannot evade the call of the law, the open-ended nature of language provides the opportunity for 'something we might still call agency', as Butler puts it, 'the repetition of an originary subordination for another purpose, one whose future is partially open' (ES: 38).

As we shall see, there are ways of responding to hate speech that will prevent its intended injurious effects from taking place, although, as before, this does not mean that hate-speakers are not responsible for their utterances. Indeed, Butler accepts that there are some cases in which it will 'probably' be necessary to prosecute the utterers of race hate, anti-gay remarks, etc. (ES: 34, 50) (although it is not entirely clear as to what or who exactly is being prosecuted in such cases). Indeed, in the absence of sovereign speaking subjects and effective performatives, how is it possible to prosecute cases in which hateful language or discourse have been deployed?

VIOLENCE IN COURT

Since the law is not an objective arbiter, Butler advocates responding to hate speech in ways that will avoid recourse to legal measures. Indeed, in her analyses of race hate and the legal prosecution of 'sexual obscenity', Butler reveals troubling anomalies that strengthen her case for seeking alternatives to legal redress. In *R.A.V. vs. Saint Paul*, a burning cross was placed on a black family's lawn by a white teenager. Butler notes that the lawyers defending the act co-opt the discursive violence they are supposed to be adjudicating, while the black family who were threatened by the burning cross are criminalized by the defending lawyers. (Butler draws some instructive parallels with the Rodney King case. See her article, 'Endangered/Endangering: Schematic Racism and White Paranoia' (1993).) These are powerful enough arguments, but Butler's own 'case' against the law hinges on the lawyers' defence of cross-burning as an act of free speech, which therefore qualifies for protection under the First Amendment to the US Constitution. Rather than constituting an act of destruction, it was argued that the burning cross expressed an, admittedly controversial and potentially offensive, viewpoint. For this reason, the act was not proscribed as 'fighting words' (a threatening utterance that has no content) but instead was protected as 'free speech'.

Matters are altogether different when it comes to sexual representations. While Butler insists on the potential failure of performatives and the scenes of agency that may open up as a consequence, advocates of censorship such as Andrea Dworkin, Matsuda and MacKinnon assume that sexual representations in some sense perform what they depict. In her discussion of MacKinnon's *Only Words* (1993), Butler argues that MacKinnon construes pornography as a kind of hate speech that has the power to enact what it names: by conflating pictures and words, as well as words and actions, MacKinnon concludes that pornographic representations have the power to enact what they depict and should therefore be censored (ES: 67). Butler, on the other hand, regards pornographic representations as 'phantasmatic', unreal and unrealizable allegories of impossible sexuality that have no power to wound. Characterizing pornography as 'the text of gender's unreality', Butler argues that 'pornography charts a domain of unrealizable positions that hold sway over the social reality of gender positions, but do not, strictly speaking, constitute that reality; indeed, it is their failure to constitute it that gives the pornographic image the phantasmatic power that it has' (ES: 68).

If pornography's power is phantasmatic rather than real, there is little sense in prosecuting such representations (or rather, their representers), and Butler calls for a feminist non-literal reading and redeployment of pornographic texts and the 'impossible' sexuality they depict (ES: 69). (But in *Bodies* Butler insists that there is no distinction between the phantasmatic and the real. See Chapter 3, this volume, pp. 83–4 and BTM: 59.) Since it does not necessarily follow that such texts are efficacious performatives, and since censoring a single text will not abolish it or other texts like it, Butler claims that it is more effective to engage in the difficult work of reading such texts against themselves while conceding that 'the performativity of the text is not under sovereign control'. Far from it in fact, since, as Butler points out, 'if the text acts once it can act again, and possibly against its prior act. This raises the possibility of *re*signification as an alternative reading of performativity and of politics' (ES: 69).

We will return to resignification shortly, but at this stage you might be asking yourself why a pornographic text is vulnerable to subversive recitation while a burning cross is not. It is certainly the case that racist terms such as 'nigger' have been 'reclaimed' by some speakers and groups of speakers (although it is a term that Butler shies away from in *Excitable Speech*), but in the context of hate speech it is important to distinguish between violent racist *acts* and violent racist *speech acts*. This does not necessarily mean that the act of burning a cross is not vulnerable to subversive redeployment, but left-thinking liberals would presumably think twice before appropriating a threatening act with a history of violence and racist oppression. According to Derrida, performative signs may be wrested from their prior usages if the structural dimension of language is emphasized over the historical (ES: 148), and, although Butler seems to endorse this position, she also acknowledges the significance of the historicity of the sign (ES: 57). Indeed, in the Introduction to *Excitable Speech*, Butler accepts that language cannot be purged of its history and that prior usages are important in determining the meaning of signs: 'There is no purifying language of its traumatic residue, and no way to work through trauma except through the arduous effort it takes to direct the course of its repetition' (ES: 38). We shall see how repetitions may be 'directed' in due course.

We saw that the defending lawyers in *R.A.V. vs. Saint Paul* argued that the burning cross was a speech act expressing a point of view, which meant that it qualified for protection under the First Amendment to the US Constitution. In contrast, the sexual representations to which Dworkin, MacKinnon and Matsuda, among others, object are *not* deemed to be utterances but acts of violence, and accordingly they do not qualify for First Amendment protection. Butler is troubled by what she regards as 'the arbitrary and tactical use of obscenity law' for the purposes of restricting African-American cultural production and lesbian and gay self-representation. It seems that the law cannot decide whether saying is doing, or doing is saying, and there are ideological agendas behind this inconsistent treatment of race hate and sexual representation. Once again, this leads her to insist on the productive gap between saying and doing (ES: 75). Acknowledging that, in certain cases, 'saying' *can* lead to harmful 'doing', Butler asserts that 'the ritual chain of hateful speech cannot be effectively countered by means of censorship' (ES: 102). This is not just because of the resident anomalies and violences of the law, but also because censorship is a simplified response to the complex workings of discourse and the law. One aspect of this complexity is the production and preservation of what is supposedly prohibited and proscribed.

MILITARY MELANCHOLIA

In fact we encountered the idea that prohibition is productive in both *Gender Trouble* and *Bodies That Matter*, and Butler continues to explore the productivity of prohibition in the third chapter of *Excitable Speech*, 'Contagious Word. Paranoia and "Homosexuality" in the Military'. The word 'homosexuality' in the chapter title is placed within inverted commas in order to signal that it is a construct rather than a pre-discursive ontological essence. Indeed, homosexuality as it emerges in *Excitable* is simultaneously produced and proscribed by military and governmental authorities, which *require* 'homosexuality' in order to maintain the cohesion of the straight male community. It is in this sense that military discourse is melancholic, since it preserves an apparently forbidden cathexis in what Butler calls the simultaneous production and restriction of the term (i.e. 'homosexuality') (ES: 105).

In her discussion of military discourse, the law and the production of homosexuality, Butler draws on three works by Freud, 'On the Mechanism of Paranoia' (1911), *Civilisation and Its Discontents* (1930) and *Totem and Taboo: Some Points of Agreement Between the Mental Lives of Savages and Neurotics* (1913). In 'On the Mechanism of Paranoia' Freud argues that the repression of homosexual desire leads to the production of social feeling, while *Civilisation and Its Discontents* analyzes how desires are preserved in the very structure of renunciation, so that prohibition is an action that is libidinally invested. In the context of the army, Butler claims that the act of renouncing homosexual desire is a way of *preserving* that desire: homosexuality is therefore never renounced, but, as Butler puts it, is 'retained in the speaking of the prohibition' (ES: 117).

Clearly this is not acknowledged by military authorities, which seek to prevent homosexual utterances that they deem equivalent to sexual acts. *Totem and Taboo* provides Butler with a framework for her discussion of the metaphor of contagion that is deployed in military discourses, where verbal acknowledgements of homosexuality are figured as a disease, specifically, Aids. In the eyes of the military and the government, words with a homosexual content possess the properties of contagious fluids that 'communicate' in the same way that the Aids virus does (ES: 110). Clearly these communications are deemed to be more than 'only words', as in military and governmental discourses language is figured as possessing the characteristics of a deadly virus that may 'act on' the listener. Coming out is therefore construed as a sexual act and, as Butler puts it, utterances that *represent* a disposition or a practice are conflated with that disposition and practice, 'a becoming, a transitivity that depends on and institutes the collapse of the distinction between speech and conduct' (ES: 112).

On the other hand, Butler continues to insist on the disjunction between speech and conduct, and she argues that, even if utterances can be construed as acts, it does not necessarily follow that utterances *act on* the listener in predetermined ways (ES: 113). Furthermore, although coming out is forbidden in military contexts, we know that official discourses are *themselves* active in preserving the desires that they outlaw. '[P]rohibition becomes the displaced site of satisfaction for the "instinct" or desire that is prohibited, an occasion for the reliving of the instinct under the rubric of the condemning law', Butler writes. '[D]esire is *never* renounced, but becomes preserved and reasserted in the very structure of renunciation' (ES: 117). Far from consigning homosexuality to silence, homosexuality is retained in the very structure of the prohibition itself and, by transforming homosexual desire into a sense of guilt, military discourses *produce* the figure of the homosexual along with what Butler calls 'the masculinist citizen' (ES: 121).

Ascribing agency and contagion (or agency *in* contagion) to the homosexual word means that the homosexual subject is defined as assaultive and dangerous. It would seem that military discourse possesses the performative power to bring what it names into being (i.e. the figure of the homosexual), and Butler concedes that, on a more general level, utterances are sometimes effective. All the same, what Butler calls 'a discursive production of homosexuality, a talking about, a writing about, and institutional recognition of homosexuality' is not the same as the desire that is referred to: homosexuality is *discursive*, but it is not referential; in other words, *discourse about desire is not synonymous with desire itself*, so that sign and referent remain distinct (ES: 125), while to claim that language *acts* is not the same as saying that it *acts on* someone (ES: 113).

Butler calls for a 'disjoining' of homosexuality from the cultural figures by which it is represented in a dominant discourse, where it is still widely aligned with contagion and disease. The possibility of such a disjoining represents what Butler calls 'the future of our life within language', whereby the signifiers of homosexuality are open to contestation and democratic rearticulation. Again, resignification and the open temporality of signs that are never finally semantically determined will provide conditions of agency and possibility within discourses that are inevitably 'impure', and these features of language inform the suggestions Butler makes for alternatives to censorship and other legal measures.

AGAINST CENSORSHIP

Butler argues that, to utilize authorities/regimes such as the law by calling for the censorship of, for example, sexual representations, would effectively strengthen those institutions as well as sanctioning the violent anti-gay/racist discourses they might deploy in the course of their proscriptions. For this reason it is better to avoid censorship altogether. As an alternative to legal redress, Butler suggests that it is more effective to exploit the open temporality of signs that may be wrested from their prior contexts and made to resignify in unexpected, subversive ways. As in *Bodies That Matter*, in the concluding chapter of *Excitable Speech* Butler argues that pre-eminently *iterable* signs are always vulnerable to expropriation and radical re-citation. Once again she engages Derrida's characterization of signs as repeatable, relatively autonomous and therefore not inevitably bound to their historical contexts. In her considerations of historicity, context and convention, Butler sets Derrida's theories of the sign against Austin's descriptions of language, and the analyses of social convention of French anthropologist and sociologist, Pierre Bourdieu (1930–) in *Language and Symbolic Power* (1991) and *The Logic of Practice* (1990). Whereas Austin insists on the binding force of convention and Bourdieu characterizes social institutions as static entities, Derrida claims that contexts are 'illimitable', while institutions are, like language, subject to social transformation (ES: 147). Conventions and institutions can be broken with, performatives may 'fail' to enact what they set out to name, and these failures may be mobilized in the service of a radical politics of resignification. Indeed, Butler sees Derrida as 'offer[ing] a way to think performativity in relation to transformation, to the break with prior contexts, with the possibility of inaugurating contexts yet to come' (ESP: 151–2). Whereas Bourdieu forecloses agency by claiming that performative utterances are only effective when they are spoken by those in power (ES: 156), Derrida makes failure the mark of his mark, so that what Butler calls 'the *expropriability* of the dominant, "authorized" discourse' makes it vulnerable to radical resignification and redeployment (ES: 157).

Now Butler wants to know what happens when oppressed groups of people start laying claim to terms such as 'justice' and 'democracy', from which they have hitherto been excluded. She suggests that there is a performative power in appropriating the terms by which one has been abused, which 'depletes' the term of its degradation and converts it into an affirmation: 'queer', 'black' and 'women' are the examples she gives here (ES: 158). While Butler continues to insist on the subversive possibilities of appropriation, we have seen that she does not overlook the significance of the sedimented usages of the sign, i.e. the meanings signs may have accrued and the significance of these prior usages. Although history is not semantically determining, Butler accepts that prior meanings are still important in constituting both social and physical identities (ES: 159). However, she also asserts that 'sullied' terms are vulnerable to unexpected innocence and she continues to emphasize the productive lability of the speech acts which may be recontextualized so that they take on unexpected meanings. This is what Butler calls 'the political promise of the performative, one that positions the performative at the center of a politics of hegemony, one that offers an unanticipated political future for deconstructive thinking' (ES: 161). The open temporality of the sign means that insults and derogatory names may become the occasions for

counter-mobilizations and radical reappropriations, and Butler advocates the risky practice of appropriating potentially harmful terms:
'[i]nsurrectionary speech becomes the necessary response to injurious
language', she insists, 'a risk taken in response to being put at risk, a
repetition in language that forces change' (ES: 163; see also WIC,
where Butler reiterates the political necessity of risk).

In a recent interview, Butler herself provides a practical example
of the linguistic risk-taking she advocates here as she describes an
encounter with a 'kid' in Berkeley who leaned out of a window and
asked her whether she was a lesbian. Butler replied in the affirmative,
noting that her interlocutor, who clearly meant the question as an
insult, was taken aback by her proud appropriation of the term. 'It
was a very powerful thing to do', Butler explains:

> It wasn't that I authored that term: I received the term and gave it back; I
> replayed it, reiterated it . . . It's as if my interrogator were saying, 'Hey, what
> do we do with the word *lesbian*? Shall we still use it?' And I said 'Yeah, let's
> use it *this* way!' Or it's as if the interrogator hanging out the window were
> saying 'Hey, do you think the word *lesbian* can only be used in a derogatory
> way on the street?' And I said 'No, it can be claimed on the street! Come join
> me!' We were having a negotiation.
>
> (CTS: 760)

Here Butler expropriates and subversively resignifies oppressive
language, exemplifying the practice of positive appropriation she advocates in *Excitable*. By claiming the word 'lesbian' in her encounter with
the Berkeley 'kid' and by acknowledging that there are a number of
different ways in which the term can be understood or played, Butler
robs the situation of its violent potential so that as she puts it at the
end of this description of iterability-in-practice, 'No, it doesn't have
to be hate speech'. However, a number of important questions remain:
can a single speaker wrest a term such as 'lesbian' from its prior
contexts in order to make it signify in unexpectedly 'innocent' ways?
If there is no doer behind the deed, then what sort of an agent will
effect such a recontextualization, and must resignifications be recognized as such? Furthermore, if resignifications take place within
discourse and the law, then how do we know that they are not *themselves* the products of the law? Why would we want to appropriate the
terms that have oppressed us in the past, particularly if such terms

cannot be 'purified' of their sedimented histories? Could it be that, like the strategic essentialism from which Butler *strategically* distances herself, such appropriations will strengthen rather than undermine dominant discourse?

CONCLUDING QUESTIONS

These are challenging questions and, although a number of them are raised or acknowledged in *Excitable Speech*, in characteristically open-ended fashion they are not satisfactorily resolved (although by now we might think there was something wrong if they were). Perhaps the question of the subject or the agent of speech has the most serious implications for Butler's ongoing deconstruction of identity categories and her theorizations of language in *Excitable Speech*. If there is no prior subject, no doer behind the deed, then who or what is it that effects the kind of linguistic and semantic reallocations that Butler exemplifies in the interview quoted above? Would it be possible for me as a 'subject-effect' to make the autonomous and unilateral decision that 'lesbian' is now an affirmative term, particularly if my interlocutor is not in agreement with me? It is entirely possible that the 'kid' left her or his brief encounter with Butler with an unaltered view of the term 'lesbian' and those who identify as lesbians, and it could be argued that how we judge the efficacy of Butler's appropriative strategy depends at least in part on the kid's response.

In that case, it would seem that, even if contexts are not binding, semantic consensus is still important in the successful redeployment of performatives. We may accept with Derrida and Butler that sign and referent are not intrinsically connected, but in spite of this arbitrary link it is still not clear how it is possible to rematch signs with alternative referents. Just as Austin's man on the waterfront cannot come along and name a ship *Mr Stalin* once it has been named something else, speakers cannot single-handedly alter the meaning of signs. If Butler uses the term 'lesbian' in one way, and the Berkeley kid still understands it in another, what exactly has been achieved? According to Butler's own reading of Althusser, the Berkeley kid might continue to 'call' Butler a lesbian in a way that is wounding and insulting, and even though Butler may not choose to recognize herself in the interpellation, the call of the kid will still have the performative force to subject and subjectivate Butler. In other words, *Excitable Speech* does not provide a clear idea of how interpellatives may be replayed or their meanings altered.

Butler accepts that words cannot be metaphorically purified of their historicity, even though she celebrates what she calls 'the vulnerability of sullied terms to unexpected innocence'. However, she gives little sense of exactly *how* sullied terms may be made 'innocent' again, and indeed she herself seems reluctant to deploy such terms in *Excitable Speech*: whereas the word 'queer' has been widely appropriated so that in many contexts it is no longer a term of abuse, there is a question mark over 'nigger', which is still a verbal insult when used in certain contexts by certain speakers. Butler's reluctance to resignify this term (which is used only once in *Excitable Speech*) may be symptomatic of her hesitation as to whether words *do* wound and her uncertainty as to how radical resignifications are effected. In that case, it would be possible to describe *Excitable Speech* itself as a failed performative since ultimately it does not enact the theory it describes.

A further question, already raised, is whether we *want* to effect the appropriations and resignifications Butler advocates, since these acts, which might look subversive on the surface, may be no more than the effects of power. Why should we retain or remain attached to the terms that subordinate us, and how will it be possible to distinguish subversive repetitions from repetitions that merely strengthen existing power structures? The question of the subject's attachment to subjection is the focus of *The Psychic Life of Power*, published in the same year as *Excitable Speech*, in which Butler returns to the issues of subjection, subjectivation and *self*-subjection in response to the call of the law.

SUMMARY

Does language enact what it names? Do words wound? Is threatening someone or talking about hitting them the same as *actually* doing so? Should representing sex or talking about sex/sexuality be construed as 'sexual conduct'? Who decides whether representations are 'obscene' or 'pornographic', and should such representations be censored?

These are some of the questions posed in *Excitable Speech*, where once again Foucault, Althusser, Austin and Derrida provide the theoretical frameworks for Butler's analyses of language and the subject. In *Gender Trouble* and *Bodies That Matter* the subject was characterized as a performative entity, but in *Excitable* Butler argues that language is not necessarily (or indeed ever) an effective performative; in other words, it does not always enact what it names. Moreover, if we accept that the subject comes *after* rather than before the deed (an argument put forward in *Gender Trouble* and *Bodies* and reiterated here), then it will be difficult to ascertain who or what to prosecute in cases of hate speech or 'obscenity'/'pornography'. Butler is also concerned by the extent to which legal institutions are implicated in producing and circulating the 'violent'/'obscene'/'pornographic' representations they apparently aim to censor.

If we accept Nietzsche's formulation that there is no doer behind the deed, it may be difficult to see what agent or subject will bring about the semantic and linguistic changes Butler describes as necessary to the linguistic future of certain marginalized or oppressed communities. Furthermore, the idea that sullied terms are vulnerable to innocence is paradoxical, and Butler herself concedes that prior histories are significant in determining the meaning of signs. It is also not always clear as to why sullied terms should be appropriated, since such a practice may engage the subject in acts of self-subjection that effectively strengthen discourse and the law: self-subjection and the subject's attachment to the law are dealt with in *The Psychic Life of Power*.

5

THE PSYCHE

CONTEXTS

In *Excitable Speech* Butler suggested that subjects must embrace the terms that injure them, and in *The Psychic Life of Power* she similarly argues that subjects are attached to the power structures that subordinate them. Reading the psyche through Hegel, Nietzsche, Freud, Foucault and Althusser in *The Psychic Life of Power*, Butler finds that the subjects described by these philosophers are formed in the act of turning against themselves in a guilty embrace of the law which condemns them and, in so doing, constitutes them. The formation of the subject is at once a process of cancellation, overcoming and preservation (i.e. *Aufhebung*, or sublation). Since there can be no social identity without subjection, Butler argues that the subject is passionately attached to the law or the authority that subjects it. Once again, identities are taken up through repudiation, guilt and loss, and it is impossible to evade or transcend the power structures within which subject-formation occurs.

However, Butler finds potential for agency in the operations of a psyche that exceeds rather than escapes the law, and *The Psychic Life of Power* could well be described as an analysis of the power of psychic life – in other words, the psyche's potential to turn power against itself. As before, Butler brings Freudian and psychoanalytic theory to bear on her readings of Hegel, Nietzsche, Foucault and Althusser in order to describe how prohibition and repudiation are libidinally invested functions of power structures that contain the potential for their own subversion.

POWER AND THE PSYCHE

In Butler's analyses one is not born, but rather one becomes, a subject (to adapt de Beauvoir's formulation), and the way one does so is by submitting to power (PLP: 2). We have encountered the subject in previous works, and here Butler defines it as 'a critical category . . . a linguistic category, a placeholder, a structure in formation . . . the linguistic occasion for the individual to achieve and reproduce intelligibility' (PLP: 10–11). (For a useful account of the subject, see Elizabeth Grosz's entry in *Feminism and Psychoanalysis: A Critical Dictionary* (Wright 1992: 409–16). Butler does not define 'psychic' or psyche, but *Psychic* focuses on the emergence of consciousness, specifically its emergence within discourse and the law. As Butler claims in her introduction, in this context it makes sense to theorize the relationship between power and the psyche by considering the psychic form that power takes and the formation of the psyche within power structures. In doing so, Butler deploys both Foucauldian and psychoanalytic theories, not in order to synthesize them, but so that she can carry out an investigation into power and the psyche, which she claims has been neglected by theorists of Foucauldian and psychoanalytic 'schools' or orthodoxies (PLP: 3). Criticizing Foucault for neglecting the subversive potential of the psyche in his accounts of power, Butler nonetheless continues to describe power in Foucauldian terms as multiple, myriad and productive. As before, the subject is the *effect* of a prior power (PLP: 14–15), and yet power is also the *condition* of the subject without which it could not exist as an agent (and it seems that the subject *is* an agent, even though it is 'mired' in power structures) (PLP: 14). The subject does not wield power, and the agency it possesses is the effect of subordination: in other words, the subject requires power in order to be a subject, and without power there would be no potential for either subject-status or agency. The subject emerges as the effect of a prior power that it also exceeds, but power also '*acts on*' a subject that appears to (but does not) precede power (PLP: 14–15).

This line of causation is important, since, if the subject were merely the effect of power, it would be hard to see how it could subvert existing power structures. Butler insists on the subject's agency as 'the assumption of a purpose *unintended* by power, one that could not have been derived logically or historically, that operates in a relation of contingency and reversal to the power that makes it possible, to which it nevertheless belongs' (PLP: 15). The subject's relationship to power is ambivalent: it depends on power for its existence, and yet it also wields power in unexpected, potentially subversive ways. We will return to *ambivalence* and *agency* in due course.

UNHAPPY CONSCIOUSNESS

In the first chapter of *Subjects of Desire*, Butler analyzes Hegel's description of the encounter between the lord and the bondsman who labours for him, where the bondsman is motivated to work in order to know himself, even though he knows that the lord will eventually appropriate the object on which he labours. In the first chapter of *Psychic* Butler returns to Hegel's description of the relationship between the lord and his bondsman and the account of unhappy consciousness that follows (see Hegel 1807: 'Independence and dependence of self-consciousness: Lordship and Bondage', and 'Freedom of self-consciousness: Stoicism, Scepticism and the Unhappy Consciousness'). As in *Subjects*, Butler describes how the bondsman labours on an object that he knows will eventually be taken away from him by the lord, even though that object bears the bondsman's signature. The lord is thus a threat to the bondsman's autonomy, and yet, according to Butler, it is in that threat that the bondsman recognizes himself (PLP: 39). Work is for Hegel a form of desire, a wanting to be, and it is also the means through which the bondsman comes to signify and to know himself. Since the object upon which the bondsman labours is a projection of the bondsman's Self, he will come to know himself as a transient object that is always vulnerable to appropriation.

After the lord has been eventually displaced the bondsman internalizes the subjection under which he formerly laboured, resulting in a psyche that is split into lord and bondsman and a body that is split off from consciousness. The bondsman is now subjected to *himself*, a self-subjection motivated by his fear of ethical imperatives or norms, i.e. the laws he must obey. Butler traces the Hegelian subject's progression through the next stages of its phenomenological 'journey', stoicism and scepticism: now the unhappy split consciousness takes itself as its own object of scorn, so that its identity is a sort of Jekyll and Hyde-like structure of conflict and contradiction (PLP: 46). The unhappy consciousness continually berates itself, and in its stoic phase it is what Butler calls 'an incessant performer of renunciation' because it is always giving things up, including itself (PLP: 49). According to Butler, this self-renunciation is a form of negative narcissism and an 'engaged preoccupation with what is most debased and defiled about it [i.e. the subject]': in other words, the unhappy consciousness is fascinated by its own abjection, since it is through its abjection that it knows itself (PLP: 50).

Paradoxically, stoicism and self-renunciation are *pleasurable* assertions of Self, and here Hegel anticipates Freud's analyses of the law in *Civilisation and Its Discontents* (PLP: 53–4). In seeking to overcome body and pleasure, the subject asserts precisely those features *through* renunciation, so that in this stage of its development it knows itself via what Butler calls 'the sanctification of abjection' (PLP: 51). Is this the only way the subject can know itself, or are there alternatives to the self-mortification and self-renunciation Hegel describes in section four of *Phenomenology*? Butler considers this question in her account of post-Hegelian subjects and subjections.

AFTER HEGEL

Butler is particularly interested in how the forms of self-beratement Hegel describes prefigure Freudian neurosis and homosexual panic (PLP: 54), and her discussion of post-Hegelian subjects and subjections focuses on Nietzsche's *On the Genealogy of Morals*, Freud's *Civilisation and its Discontents* and Foucault's *Discipline and Punish*. These texts are connected by their descriptions of the subject's attachment to subjection and self-abnegation, specifically, the abnegation of the body or desire.

In psychoanalytic accounts of subject-formation the body is never finally subjected because prohibition is a libidinally invested activity. This is a formulation we came across in *Excitable Speech*, where, as here, Butler draws from Freud's analyses of conscience in *Civilisation*. According to Freud, desire is preserved both in and through the very act of renunciation, which means that, as in *Excitable*, 'desire is *never*

renounced, but becomes preserved and reasserted in the very structure of renunciation' (PLP: 56; ES: 117). Accordingly, the subject is
attached to subjection, since subjection itself affords a kind of pleasure, something Nietzsche recognizes in *Genealogy*, and an insight that
is picked up by Foucault in *Discipline*. There, as in *Civilisation*, the
prohibitive law produces the body it sets out to suppress, and we know
that, unlike Hegel, Foucault argues that the body does not (usually)
precede the discourses and laws that suppress it (PLP: 60). The
Foucauldian account of subjection contains the potential for agency and
subversion that appears to be absent from *Phenomenology*, leading Butler
to depart from Hegel via Foucault.

What characterizes Nietzschean, Freudian, Foucauldian and indeed
Hegelian subjects is their attachment to subjection. As we have seen,
there can be no subject without subjection, and this places the subject
in the paradoxical position of having to desire precisely that which
threatens to close its desire down (i.e. prohibition). Butler expresses
this in the following formulation that is presumably ironically repeti-
tious, since the phrase is repeated verbatim a few pages later: 'the
desire to desire is a willingness to desire precisely that which would
foreclose desire, if only for the possibility of continuing to desire'
(PLP: 61, 79). Since desire is constitutive, post-Hegelian subjects will
desire prohibition rather than not desiring anything at all, but their
attachment to subjection does not mean that they are unable to assert
their agency-within-subordination.

IN LOVE WITH THE LAW

Nietzsche and Freud theorize the operation of conscience and the production of the psyche or soul through a violent morality. In *Genealogy*,
Nietzsche distinguishes between conscience and bad conscience, defining the latter as an illness that afflicts 'man': 'I take bad conscience to
be the deep sickness to which man was obliged to succumb under the
pressure of the most fundamental of all changes – when he found himself definitively locked in the spell of society and peace', he writes
(1887: 64), and he describes how morality causes man to turn inwards
and redirect his 'wild' instincts against himself in an action that
psychoanalysts would later characterize as repression (1887: 65).

Nietzsche's subject is the effect of self-violence and a turning against
the Self precipitated by socially-imposed prohibition and morality, and

Butler draws attention to the subject's engagement in acts of self-violence. '[S]uch violence founds the subject', she notes; 'the subject who would oppose violence, even violence to itself, is itself the effect of a prior violence without which the subject could not have emerged' (PLP: 64). Nietzsche emphasizes 'the *will* of man to find himself guilty and reprehensible to a point beyond the possibility of atonement, his *will* to think himself punished without the punishment ever being commensurate with his guilt, his *will* to infect and poison things to their very depths with the problem of punishment and guilt' (1887: 73; his emphasis). Butler also notes the element of volition (or self-will) in the subject's guiltiness, but she argues that the moral self-reflexivity whereby the subject turns back upon itself turns out to be an act of self-constitution.

In the second chapter of *The Psychic Life of Power* Butler asks whether Nietzsche's 'bad conscience' precedes the subject's self-reflexive self-beratement, in other words, whether the subject is the effect of a law which precedes it. In fact, Butler claims, the subject is 'a kind of necessary fiction . . . one of the first artistic accomplishments presupposed by morality', so that it is clear that, as in *Excitable Speech,* the law fabricates this entity on which it supposedly exerts its power (PLP: 66). Crucially, Butler asserts that Nietzschean bad conscience is a trope, a metaphor, and that Nietzsche's descriptions make no ontological claims; in other words, Nietzsche is *not* positing a subject or a conscience that is prior to the law (PLP: 69). We will return to the *tropological subject* in due course, but here Butler also points out that Nietzsche's descriptions of the formation of conscience are implicated in the moral discourse he describes because the terms he uses are the effects of the formation of conscience (PLP: 77). To argue that Nietzsche's *Genealogy* is *itself* the product of bad conscience raises the question as to whether genealogical investigations can ever be separate from the power structures they describe. If it is impossible to think of the subject outside the terms of regulation, Butler's own account will be similarly discursively implicated and complicit with the law it is theorizing (PLP: 77).

Butler discerns resonances of Nietzsche's account of bad conscience in Freud's *Civilisation* as well as in his essay 'On Narcissism' (1914), both of which are concerned with the operations of conscience. In his analyses of neurosis, Freud asserts that the psyche is libidinally attached to a prohibitive agent, which itself becomes a nexus of desire. We encountered this idea in *Excitable Speech*, and in *The Psychic Life of Power* Butler reiterates the Freudian formulation that the libido is not negated when it is repressed, since the law itself is libidinally invested. At this point Butler repeats the sentence I quoted earlier: 'The desire to desire is a willingness to desire precisely what would foreclose desire, if only for the possibility of continuing to desire' (PLP: 79). As before, Butler implies that subjects want to want, and yet the object of their desire is precisely what would prevent them from wanting. Repression and desire cannot be separated, since repression itself is a libidinal activity, and far from attempting to evade the moral interdictions which are turned against it, the body sustains these interdictions in order to continue desiring (PLP: 79). Subjects desire to desire, and they will desire the law that threatens them rather than not desiring anything at all.

'[T]he ethical regulation of bodily impulse', i.e. the repression of physical desires, is *itself* a desiring activity, and in the first chapter of *Psychic* Butler also points out that the agent of the moral law is in fact its most serious transgressor (PLP: 55–6). Butler gives literary examples of bearers of the moral law who experience (sexual?) satisfaction in enforcing prohibition, but the formulation could equally well apply to former US Senator Jesse Helms, who, as we saw in Chapter 4, produces a 'pornographic' legal text in the very act of setting out to censor pornography. In *Excitable Speech* Butler also construed the military proscription of 'homosexual' utterance as paranoid, and in the second chapter of *Psychic* she returns to Freud's theorization of paranoia as a form of sublimated homosexuality (and again she cites the regulation of homosexuality in the US military as an example of preservation in renunciation) (PLP: 82). As before, disavowal and prohibition are highly productive activities that simultaneously produce and contain homosexuality by suppressing it (PLP: 80). In Freud's *Civilisation* prohibition produces the desire it prohibits, leading Butler to reassert the Nietzschean formulation that bad conscience involves Self, body and desire recoiling on themselves in 'a narcissistically nourished self-beratement' (PLP: 82).

Prohibition, self-beratement and self-punishment are necessary to the existence of the subject, and in the Freudian account of repression and prohibition the libido and the body cannot be effectively or finally repressed since prohibitive actions are *themselves* the objects of the subject's desire. There is potential for agency in psychic excess, an insight that informs Butler's critique of Foucault's omission of the excessive and resistant psyche from his account of the operations of power.

FOUCAULT'S PRISONERS

In *Discipline and Punish* Foucault describes how subject-formation operates through the discursive formation of the body. As Butler points out, 'formation' is not the same as 'causing' and 'determining' so that this Foucauldian formulation is by no means the simple reduction of the body to 'discourse'. Like the other accounts of conscience Butler has considered so far, Foucauldian subjection is a productive process, 'a kind of restriction *in* production' without which subject-formation cannot take place. Noting that the psyche, which is not synonymous with the unconscious, is omitted from Foucault's account of subjection, Butler's 'psychoanalytic criticism of Foucault' insists that it is impossible to describe subjection and subjectivation without drawing from psychoanalytic theory, since without the psyche there is no possibility of resistance. In *Discipline* Foucault describes the soul, here taken to be synonymous with the psyche, as an imprisoning effect of the power which entraps the discursively regularized body. And yet, Butler argues that the psyche exceeds and resists the normalizing discourses Foucault describes: 'Where does resistance to or in disciplinary formation take place?', she asks.

> Does the reduction of the psychoanalytically rich notion of the psyche to that of the imprisoning soul eliminate the possibility of resistance to normalization and to subject formation, a resistance that emerges precisely from the incommensurability between psyche and subject? How would we understand such resistance, and would such an understanding entail a critical rethinking of psychoanalysis along the way?
>
> (PLP: 87)

The 'possibility of resistance' is crucial to Butler's account of the subject, and she asks how Foucault can account for the psychic resistance to power if the psyche/soul as he formulates it is no more than an imprisoning effect. Conversely, by training a Foucauldian lens on psychoanalytic theory, Butler raises the question as to whether psychic resistance is an effect of power, a discursive production rather than a means of undermining power. Resistance takes place within discourse or the law, but what Butler calls a 'psychic remainder' – the element of the psyche that is 'left over', so to speak, when discursive operations have done their work – signifies the limits of normalization even while it is also clear that the unconscious does not escape the power relations by which it is structured.

Butler also raises the question of what she calls 'the problem of bodies in Foucault'. If the soul is the prison of the body as Foucault claims it is, then does this mean that a pre-existing body is acted upon by disciplinary structures? In her early article, 'Foucault and the Paradox of Bodily Inscriptions', Butler sets out the following 'paradox' in Foucault's theorizations of bodies and discourses: although Foucault asserts that bodies are discursively constructed, his descriptions of the mechanisms of legal inscription seem to presuppose that they *pre-exist* the law (FPBI: 603). Departing from (or perhaps developing) this paradox in *Psychic*, Butler argues that body and soul are discursive formations that emerge simultaneously through the sublimation of body into soul. 'Sublimation' is a psychoanalytic term describing the transformation or diversion of sexual drives into 'cultural' or 'moral' activities, and Butler uses it to describe the process whereby the body is subordinated and partly destroyed as what she calls 'the dissociated Self' emerges. (This definition of sublimation is taken from Wright 1992: 416–17.) However, Butler argues that the sublimation of body into soul or psyche leaves behind a 'bodily remainder', which exceeds the processes of normalization and survives as what Butler calls 'a kind of constitutive loss' (PLP: 92). 'The body is not a site on which a construction takes place', Butler argues; 'it is a destruction on the occasion of which a subject is formed' (PLP: 92). Once again we find ourselves in the realm of Butlerian paradox, but this is an elaboration of the paradox that is central to *Psychic*: the subject comes into being when her body is acted upon and destroyed (presumably by discourse?), which means that this is a *productive* destruction or, perhaps, a sublation or *Aufhebung*, since both the body and the psyche are simultaneously formed and destroyed within discursive structures.

The contrast between psychoanalytic and Foucauldian formulations of the subject should be clear: whereas in the former the psyche and possibly also the body, are sites of excess and possible resistance, for Foucault *all* resistance takes place within the terms of the law – indeed, resistance is an effect of the law. '[R]esistance appears as the effect of power', Butler writes, paraphrasing Foucault, 'as a part of power, its self-subversion' (PLP: 93). Even so, within the Foucauldian model of myriad and pervasive power structures, the law may be subversively reiterated and repeated in order to destabilize existing norms, and Butler asks how and in what direction it is possible to work the power relations by which subjects are worked (PLP: 100). Since the Foucauldian subject is always in the process of construction, these processes are vulnerable to repetition, and, by implication, subversion, yet Butler notes the risk of renormalization within this model of identity, and she wonders how resistance may be derived from discourse itself (PLP: 93, 94).

Once again reading Foucauldian theory through a psychoanalytic lens, Butler argues that, whereas Foucault claims that psychoanalysis sees the law as separate from desire, there can be no desire without the law that produces and sustains it. We have returned to the Freudian notion of libidinally-invested law and a prohibition that is in itself a form of desire, so that, rather than claiming that the unconscious is located outside power structures, Butler argues that power *itself* possesses an unconscious that provides the conditions for radical reiteration. It is because the injurious terms of the law by which subjects are socially constituted are vulnerable to repetition and re-iteration that subjects accept and occupy these terms. 'Called by an injurious name, I come into social being and because I have a certain inevitable attachment to my existence, because a certain narcissism takes hold of any term that confers existence, I am led to embrace the terms that injure me because they constitute me socially', Butler asserts (PLP: 104). The operations of name-calling, or interpellation, and the passionate pursuit of the law complement Butler's Foucauldian and psychoanalytic formulations, and they will be considered in the next section.

REVERSE INTERPELLATION

In *The Psychic Life of Power*, Butler once again critiques Althusser's description of effective interpellative performatives and obedient subjects who automatically turn around in response to the call of the law, and, as in *Bodies That Matter* and *Excitable Speech*, she insists that the law does not possess a divine performative power to bring what it names into being. Butler compares the policeman's 'Hey, you there!'

in Althusser's example to a religious baptism or God's naming of Peter and Moses, namings that compel the subject into social being. And yet this characterization of the divine power of naming presupposes a subject that is willing to turn around and embrace the terms by which it is called, raising the question as to whether there is an addressee prior to the address, or whether the act of naming brings the subject into being. As you would expect from previous accounts of interpellation and performativity, Butler argues the latter by suggesting that the subject is formed in the repeated act of acquitting itself of the guilt of which it is accused by the law (PLP: 118).

The dual actions of guilt and acquittal condition the subject, so that, in Althusser's account, to be a subject is synonymous with being 'bad' (PLP: 119). As before, Butler is interested in how interpellation works by failing or 'missing its mark' as she puts it in *Excitable Speech*, and in the third chapter of *The Psychic Life of Power* she emphasizes the subversive potential of unstable identities and misrecognition. Particularly if the subject is hailed by a name that is constitutive of a social identity-in-inferiority (the examples Butler gives are 'woman', 'Jew', 'queer', 'Black' and 'Chicana'), the symbolic term is exceeded by the psychic or imaginary (PLP: 96–7). Moreover, there is more than one way of 'turning around' and recognizing oneself, so that, as in *Bodies*, interpellation is not a straightforwardly effective performative that has the power to enact what it names.

Butler's psychoanalytic reading of Althusser in the fourth chapter of *Psychic* ('"Conscience Doth Make Subjects of Us All": Althusser's Subjection') reveals how the interpellative call may be exceeded, as opposed to evaded. According to Butler, Althusser's subject is passionately attached to the law that hails it since, as before, social identity can only be acquired through the guilty embrace of the law. Althusser himself provides an example of this willing pursuit of the law as, in his own account he recalls running out into the street to call the police after murdering his wife, Hélène. Althusser's proclamation of his guilt reverses the interpellative scene, so that in this instance it is the subject who calls out 'Hey, you there!' to the police in a bid for the social recognition and subject-status that will be conferred by condemnation.

Althusserian interpellation thus resembles Nietzsche's slave morality or Freud's description of conscience, and yet the account appears to posit a subject that precedes the law that hails it (PLP: 117). Focusing on Althusser's emphasis on the subject's guilty embrace of the law and her or his self-acquittal, Butler finds that there is in fact no subject that precedes the performance of this 'rite' (PLP: 119). The subject comes into being through the simultaneous actions of submission and mastery, and yet neither of these acts is performed by the subject that is the effect rather than the cause of those acts (PLP: 117). Althusser's invocation of a subject *before* the law is encountered as a grammatical problem, whereby the subject-as-cause is linguistically installed as *prior* to ideology and the call of the law; whereas Butler argues that power simultaneously acts on and activates the subject by naming it. 'To the extent that naming is an address, there is an addressee prior to the address', Butler argues, 'but given that the address is a name which creates what it names, there appears to be no "Peter" without the name "Peter"' (PLP: 111). Again, this might sound paradoxical, but in fact Butler's formulation is structurally identical to her previous reversals of cause and effect in *Gender Trouble*, *Bodies That Matter* and *Excitable Speech* where, as you will recall, there is no doer behind the deed but the 'doing' itself is everything.

As in her previous discussions of interpellation, Butler casts doubt on who or what exactly is interpellated by a law that confers social identity in subjection, and she also questions the performative efficacy of the law. The call of the law is not a divine performative, since there are ways of turning around that indicate what Butler calls 'a willing-ness *not* to be – a critical desubjectivation – in order to expose the law as less powerful than it seems' (PLP: 130). Anticipating her essay, 'What Is Critique?', which also insists on the subversive potential of giving up the claim to a coherent identity, Butler asks how it is possible to understand the desire to be as a constitutive desire, and how laws exploit subjects that allow themselves to be subordinated in order to take up their positions in society. Rather than obediently responding to the terms by which one is interpellated, a more ethical and subver-sive mode of being is, paradoxically, *failing* to be by not recognizing oneself in the call of the law (PLP: 131). The subject cannot 'be' in any coherent sense anyway, since we know from Butler's previous accounts that it is haunted by its abjected and socially unacceptable desires. Indeed, like *Gender Trouble* and *Bodies That Matter*, *Psychic* continues to insist on the melancholia of gendered and sexed identi-ties that will always and inevitably exceed the terms by which they are socially constituted.

MELANCHOLY GENDER REVISITED

How do the accounts of subjection and subjectivation Butler analyzes relate specifically to gendered and sexed identities? Earlier in *Psychic* Butler described 'a certain kind' of homosexual identity that emerges through prohibition and loss: homosexuality is cited in her description of subversive appropriation and the risks of renormalization, while 'queer' is one of the examples she gives when she discusses name-calling and interpellation in the formation of the subject. In the sixth chapter of *Psychic*, 'Melancholy Gender/Refused Identification', Butler turns her attention to gendered and sexed identities, revisiting and extending many of the arguments she formulated in *Gender Trouble* and *Bodies That Matter* and again drawing from Freud, in particular 'Mourning and Melancholia', *The Ego and the Id* and *Civilisation and Its Discontents*.

Like *Gender Trouble*, *Bodies That Matter*, and *Excitable Speech*, *Psychic* argues that prohibition and repression are constitutive of identity, and Butler specifies that what is being repressed is not just desire in general but homosexual desire (or homosexual cathexis) in particular. As in *Gender Trouble*, Butler asserts that gender is not a given but a process, masculinity and femininity are 'accomplishments', while heterosexuality is an 'achievement' (PLP: 132, 135). Now Butler asks how these processes, accomplishments and achievements come about, at what cost to the subject and to other subjects who may be oppressed and negated in the process. In order to achieve a coherent heterosexual identity something has to be given up and, as before, what is relinquished is the primary homosexual cathexis that characterizes the pre-oedipal id (see Chapter 2, pp. 54–6). Prohibition, repudiation and loss form the basis of heterosexual ego formation, and both heterosexuals and homosexuals live in a heterosexual culture of gender melancholy where the loss of primary homosexual attachments may not be grieved (PLP: 139). Grief is not just a metaphor in *Psychic* and Butler draws out the parallels between Freud's descriptions of psychic loss in 'Mourning and Melancholia' and a contemporary heterosexual culture in which lost homosexual attachments may only be mourned with difficulty (PLP: 138). Butler regards this cultural inability as symptomatic of the lack of a public forum and language with which to mourn 'the seemingly endless number of deaths' from 'the ravages of AIDS' (PLP: 138). Although this is a poignant argument, the elision of metaphorical and real mourning might be taken to imply that the heterosexual subject is aware of what she or he has 'lost' but is unable or unwilling to acknowledge and declare it.

All the same, Butler is developing one of *Gender Trouble*'s most powerful contentions – that heterosexuality emerges from a repudiated homosexuality that is preserved in the very structure of that repudiation. Abjected homosexual cathexes do not simply disappear, and both *Excitable Speech* and earlier chapters of *The Psychic Life of Power* have prepared the ground for Butler's assertion that repudiation and prohibition actually *require* homosexuality in order to constitute themselves. Far from obliterating homosexuality, it is sustained by the very structures that prohibit it. '[H]omosexuality is *not* abolished but preserved, though preserved precisely in the prohibition on homosexuality', Butler insists (PLP: 142).

> [R]enunciation requires the very homosexuality that it condemns, not as its external object, but as its own most treasured source of sustenance. The act of renouncing homosexuality thus paradoxically strengthens homosexuality, but it strengthens homosexuality precisely as the power of renunciation.
>
> (PLP: 143)

Butler's situating of homosexuality at the heart of a homophobic and 'homosexually panicked' culture is of obvious political significance, as what is considered abject and unacceptable is posited as the source of heterosexual identity (although of course Butler does not formulate the idea in terms of 'sources'). Gender identity is 'acquired' through the repudiation of homosexual attachments, and the abjected same-sex object of desire is installed in the ego as a melancholic identification, so that I can only be a woman to the extent that I have desired a woman, and I can only be a man to the extent that I have desired a man. Because heterosexual identity is founded on prohibited desire for members of the same sex, to desire a member of the same sex as an adult is to 'panic' gender or, in other words, to place an apparently coherent and stable heterosexual identity at risk by revealing that it is in fact far from stable or coherent (PLP: 136).

The heterosexual subject's homosexual desire is sublimated rather than destroyed, while disavowal and repudiation structure the 'performance' of gender. Performative gender was discussed in Chapter 3, and in *Psychic* Butler seems to conflate performativity, performance and psychotherapy as she argues that what is 'acted out' in these 'gender performances' is the unresolved grief of repudiated homosexuality (PLP: 146). As in *Gender Trouble* and *Bodies That Matter*, Butler focuses on 'cross-gendered identification', or drag, as a paradigm for thinking about homosexuality, since drag is an allegory of heterosexual melancholy in which the (male) drag performer takes on the feminine gender he has repudiated as a possible object of love. Extending this paradigm to gender identity in general, Butler asserts that 'the "truest" lesbian melancholic is the strictly straight woman, and the "truest" gay male melancholic is the strictly straight man' (PLP: 146–7). In other words, heightened or exaggerated 'straight' identity is symptomatic of repudiated homosexual desire in a culture of heterosexual melancholy, where repudiated desires 'return' as what Butler calls 'hyperbolic identifications' (PLP: 147).

The homosexual melancholic may be characterized by a different kind of loss, this time not a psychic one, but the real loss of people who have died from Aids and who remain ungrieved in a heterosexist, anti-gay culture that does not permit the mourning of these deaths. Homosexual identities may also be founded on a refused heterosexual cathexis that resembles heterosexual melancholia, but, although Butler asserts the political promise of what she calls 'gay melancholia' (PLP: 147), she also argues that refused heterosexual cathexis may leave heterosexuality intact by missing the opportunity to expose its weaknesses and fissures (PLP: 148). Butler accordingly affirms the political potential of acknowledging melancholy and loss by giving up all claims to ontological coherence and embracing, rather than repudiating, sexed and gendered 'alterity'.

AFFIRMATIVE MELANCHOLIA

Previous chapters have emphasized the importance of melancholia to Butler's theories, and the idea is similarly central to *Psychic*, where it is argued that melancholia initiates representation as well as constituting a means of representation in itself. Without loss and the resulting melancholia there would be no need for the metaphorical description of the ego in psychoanalytic theory, since it is melancholia that both necessitates and facilitates that description. Moreover, melancholia and, for that matter, the ego, are tropes that are rendered in topographical terms – in other words, the metaphors used by psychoanalysts to represent the ego and melancholia are spatial. The most prominent among these tropes is that of the ego turning against itself, and Butler argues that the turn precipitated by loss and the ensuing melancholia are constitutive of an ego that does not exist prior to the turn (PLP: 171). It is loss that necessitates the description of the psychic 'land-scape', since, if the ego were not 'impaired' in this way, there would be no need for psychoanalytic theory and its metaphorical renditions of psychic life. Melancholia initiates psychic life and, by exceeding the power structures in which subjects are formed, it presents the possibility for subversion and agency. At least part of this 'excess' is ontological, since the melancholic subject is neither self-identical nor singular. In 'Mourning and Melancholia' the ego takes itself as an object and directs its violent anger against itself, an action that has charac-terized the accounts of the ego Butler has discussed. Now Butler argues that melancholia is cultivated by the state and internalized by citizens who are not aware of their relationship to an authority that conceals itself. And yet, even though it would seem that melancholia is an effect of power, there are ways of deploying the subject's self-violence and constitutive melancholia to subversive ends.

'Bhabha argues that melancholia is not a form of passivity, but a form of revolt that takes place through repetition and metonymy', Butler states, referring to the postcolonial critic Homi Bhabha. Following Bhabha's insight she asserts that aggressive melancholia can be 'marshalled' in the service of mourning and of life by killing off the critical agency or superego and turning the ego's 'turned back' aggression outwards (PLP: 190–1). There are forms of melancholia that do not involve the violent self-beratement described by Hegel, Nietzsche and so on, and Butler argues that acknowledging the trace of loss that inaugurates the subject's emergence will lead to its psychic survival. Following Derrida, Butler insists that recognizing one's constitutive melancholia will involve accepting one's Otherness, since melancholia is a process in which the other is installed as an identifi-cation in the ego (PLP: 195–6). The notion of ontological autonomy must therefore be given up as a fiction. 'To claim life . . . is to contest the righteous psyche, not by an act of will, but by submission to a sociality and linguistic life that makes such acts possible, one that exceeds the bounds of the ego and its "autonomy"', writes Butler; 'to persist in one's being means to be given over from the start to social terms that are never fully one's own' (PLP: 197). This echoes Butler's contention in *Excitable Speech* that the subject is constituted by inter-pellatives it did not choose, and in the concluding pages of *Psychic* Butler reiterates her point that interpellation works by failing, since it never fully constitutes the subject it 'hails'. All the same, the subject's relationship to interpellation and power remains ambivalent, since the 'call' of the law brings the subject into being by subjecting it.

The ambivalent Self marked by loss is tenuous at best, but agency lies in giving up any claim to coherence or self-identity by submitting to interpellation and subversively *mis*recognizing the terms by which we are hailed. Such refusals and misrecognitions take place within the power structures that subject and control us, and this might lead us to question how far submission is a means of agency and whether it is possible to recognize it as such. Butler has returned to these questions in recent discussions of mourning, melancholia and the onto-logical risks of self-incoherence in her two lectures, 'What Is Critique?' and *Antigone's Claim*, along with the co-authored book *Contingency, Hegemony, Universality*.

SUMMARY

In *The Psychic Life of Power* Butler deploys psychoanalytic, Foucauldian and Althusserian theoretical paradigms (among others) to discuss the subject's relation to power. The subject is passionately attached to the law that both subjects and constitutes it, and it exists in an ambivalent rela-tion to power structures that it desires rather than not desiring at all. Butler criticizes Foucault for leaving the psyche out of his accounts of power, the soul and the body, and she asserts that there is potential for subversive excess in a psyche that is never fully determined by the laws that subject it. Furthermore, the interpellative 'calls' of the law described by Althusser need not be sovereign or effective, and Butler discerns further potential for subversion in the failure of these performatives.

If it is acknowledged, melancholia itself may be the occasion for affir-mation and subversion and, although Butler once again characterizes sexed/gendered identities as arising from primary loss or foreclosure, she argues that acknowledging the trace of the Other is the only way the subject will become anything at all. Agency lies in giving up any claim to self-coherence, while risking one's ontological status may constitute a means of successful revolt.

AFTER BUTLER

Butler's theoretical contestations of the subject have opened up critical debates on identity, gender, sex and language, facilitating new directions for feminist theory, queer theory and philosophy (among many other areas too numerous to list). Her influence within feminist theory and queer theory has been crucial, although in the first chapter of this book we saw that Butler makes no claim to be an 'inaugurator' or 'founder' of queer theory (which of course does not have one). While a recent reviewer of the 1999 edition of *Subjects of Desire* has identified Butler as 'the most famous feminist philosopher in the United States', others regard her as the queer theorist par excellence, and *Gender Trouble* is seen by many as the book that started it all. So, for example, philosopher Lois McNay claims that Butler's work has influenced feminist understandings of gender identity (1999: 175), while Jonathan Dollimore calls Butler 'the most brilliantly eclectic theorist of sexuality in recent years' (1996: 533).

It must be said that Butler's theories have generated as much hostility as adulation and, judging by a number of recent critiques and criticisms, it would seem that the debates arising from her work have by no means been 'resolved'. The title of this chapter is somewhat misleading in this respect, since it implies that 'Butler' was an event that occurred and has finished, leaving other critics and thinkers to deal with the aftermath before deciding where to go next. To talk in terms of 'After Butler' erroneously implies some kind of closure, whereas Butler continues to maintain an active, dialectical relationship with her own texts as well as with those of other critical thinkers. At the same time, her influence on a diverse array of theoretical fields has certainly been enormous: a glance at Eddie Yeghiayan's exhaustive bibliography of Butler's works and those which reference her (there are literally hundreds of the latter), reveals the extent of her influence in, among other fields, queer theory, feminist theory, film studies, literary studies, sociology, politics and philosophy.

Rather than attempting to describe what happened 'After Butler', this concluding chapter will give a very brief survey of her recent work, along with a discussion of specific ways in which her thought has been influential. Finally, I will glimpse at forthcoming works by Butler and the critical fields in which she is currently making the theoretical interventions that continue to gain her notoriety as a thinker and theorist.

WHAT'S LEFT OF BUTLER?

What is the political importance of theory and what is the political role of the intellectual (if she or he has one)? Can existing laws be subverted and, if so, what sort of an agent will bring about that subversion? Is it possible to adopt a critical relation to the norms that form us? Is democracy a political project with 'realization' as its aim, and what would be the effects of such a political closure? Conversely, what is the outcome of a *lack* of closure? Should people currently living on the margins of social structures campaign for assimilation or should they continue to exist in a more critical and oblique, if a necessarily more painful, relation to the institutions by which they are rejected but simultaneously constituted?

These are some of the issues Butler raises in three recent works, 'What Is Critique?', *Contingency, Hegemony, Universality* and *Antigone's Claim: Kinship Between Life and Death*, all published in 2000, while a recent interview, 'Changing the Subject: Judith Butler's Politics of Radical Resignification', provides responses, if not answers, to some of these questions. Butler's recent works continue to destabilize subject-categories and norms, suggesting radical resignificatory alternatives that will undermine the law by exposing its limits. Butler's writing has always been implicitly political in its focus, but her later works tend to emphasize the political impetus underlying theories that some readers and critics have considered to be arcane, abstract and disengaged from 'material realities' (see below). (For an example of Butler's explicitly political writing see, for example, the early article 'Contingent Foundations: Feminism and the Question of Post-modernism' where Butler theorizes the subject via a discussion of the Gulf War.) In the Preface to the 1999 Anniversary edition of *Gender Trouble*, Butler makes a point of asserting that she has revised her theories in the light of her political engagements; in particular, she claims that her work with the International Gay and Lesbian Human Rights Commission has compelled her to rethink the meaning of the term 'universality', while her involvement with a progressive psychoanalytic journal, *Studies in Gender and Sexuality*, has added what some would call a 'practical' dimension to her psychoanalytic thinking.

In *What's Left of Theory?* (2000), a collection of critical essays, Butler and her co-editors raise the question of the political uses of theory and literature. The editors pun repetitively on the word 'left' as they ask whether what they call 'a politically reflective literary analysis' has left theory behind, and whether theory must be left behind in order for a politically left literary analysis to emerge (WLT: x, xii). Apart from the fifth and sixth chapters of *Bodies That Matter*, literature and the literary do not play a particularly prominent role in Butler's texts, and when she does engage in literary analysis it is usually to under-score a political or theoretical point. All the same, the questions raised in the Preface to *What's Left of Theory?* could equally apply to 'philos-ophy', which is where we might tentatively situate Butler's work if we had to. Is philosophy political, and what are the political uses of philosophy? Or, on the other hand, must the political left leave philosophy behind in order to effect a more practical engagement with the world?

In answer to these questions it could be said that the connections between politics, philosophy and theory (and, for that matter, litera-ture) are implicit in Butler's insistence that the subject should take up a critical relation to governing discourses and norms. 'What Is Critique?', *Contingency, Hegemony, Universality* and *Antigone's Claim* offer various perspectives on obedience, assimilation and resistance to authority. In 'What is Critique? An Essay on Foucault's Virtue', which was the Raymond Williams Lecture delivered at Cambridge University in May 2000, Butler describes how current ontological and epistemo-logical limits may be challenged through what she, following Foucault, calls 'the art of voluntary insubordination' (WIC: 12). Similarly, in her contributions to *Contingency, Hegemony, Universality*, a sequence of exchanges with two other theorists, Ernesto Laclau and Slavoj Žižek, Butler continues to affirm that subversively laying claim to oppressive terms will subvert hegemonic structures by exposing their limits, while in *Antigone's Claim*, the Wellek Library Lectures given in California in 1998, Sophocles' protagonist, Antigone, provides a literary example of this subversive, critical relation to existing laws and norms.

From her earliest writing to the present, Butler has engaged in an ongoing destabilization of subject-categories and the discursive structures within which they are formed, a critical exercise that is undertaken not merely for its own sake but in order to expose the limitations, contingencies and instabilities of existing norms. Butler continues these interrogations and enquiries in these three recent texts, although it is part of her political project *not* to supply answers to the difficult and troubling questions that she poses.

INFLUENCE

Even theorists who do not agree with Butler's formulations of the subject, the body, politics and language, acknowledge the impact that her ideas have had in a broad range of critical and theoretical fields. The 'Butler' entry in the *Blackwells Biographical Dictionary of Twentieth-Century Philosophers* describes performativity as the sine qua non (i.e. the indispensable condition) of postmodern feminism, and it notes the importance of Butler's work in feminist theory, lesbian and gay theory, psychoanalysis and race studies (Shildrick 1996). For example, the feminist philosopher Susan Bordo regards *Gender Trouble*'s 'postmodern' interventions into theorizations of gender as 'enormously insightful . . . and pedagogically useful' as a framework for exploring self-construction, while Butler's exposures of the workings of hetero-centrism and essentialism are 'deft' and 'brilliant' (Bordo 1993: 290). McNay agrees that Butler's ideas have been important in opening up new critical and theoretical terrains for feminism, and she suggests that, more than any other feminist theorist, Butler has pushed feminist theory beyond the polarities of the essentialist debate in her elaborations of gender identity as deeply entrenched but not immutable (McNay 1999: 175). Although Bordo and McNay disagree with Butler in significant respects, both of them acknowledge the importance of theories that deconstruct and destabilize essentialist, normative and naturalist assumptions about 'woman'.

As McNay points out, Butler's theorizations of identity as dialectic have been enormously influential in areas of study other than feminist theory, even when her ideas are disputed (1999: 177). Dollimore, who theorizes 'sexual dissidence', acknowledges Butler's brilliant eclecticism (although this might be a back-handed compliment), but he thinks some of her descriptions are ahistorical and 'hopelessly wrong' (1996: 533–5). All the same, Butler's interrogations of foundationalism and essentialism are important for queer theory's anti-identity critiques (O'Driscoll 1996: 31) and its resistance to regimes of the normal (Warner 1993: xxvi). Butler's characterization of homosexual and heterosexual identities as unstable, shifting processes repeatedly occurring over time and her theorizations of melancholic sex and gender identities constitute major theoretical *coups*. Her theories effectively reveal the 'contingent foundations' of all identity categories, and the contention that what heterosexuality is (unknowingly) contingent upon is its abjected 'Other' – homosexuality – constitutes an effective challenge to anti-gay feeling and heterocentrism. However, Dollimore worries that Butler characterizes heterosexuality as paranoid, and gay desire is seen as incomplete unless it is subversively installed within heterosexuality (Dollimore 1996: 534–5).

Butler's destabilizations of identity have been deployed in other theoretical arenas in which 'the unitary subject' has come under scrutiny. In 'Diaspora and Hybridity: Queer Identities and the Ethnicity Model', Alan Sinfield draws out the connections between Bhabha's descriptions of mimicry and the performative identities Butler theorizes (1996: 282–3). Notwithstanding Sinfield's reservations about the political efficacy of mimicry, his comparison demonstrates the broad theoretical application of the notion that identities are unstable and imitative (although it should be noted that Bhabha's *Location of Culture* came out in the same year as *Gender Trouble*, so that again Butler can by no means be identified as the 'source' of such ideas). Sociologist Vikki Bell's article, 'Mimesis as Cultural Survival: Judith Butler and Anti-Semitism', also brings performativity into the arena of race, as Bell suggests that the emphasis on mimesis in Butler's work in particular and feminist theory in general can be traced to philosophical responses to anti-Semitism after the Second World War. By focusing on mimesis as 'cultural survival', Bell links Butler's work on gender to theorizations of ethnicity and race/racism, thus 'forc[ing] attention to the specific historical and political context within which mimetic behaviour and identity performance takes place', as Bell puts it (1999a: 134). This is an important argument since ahistoricism and decontextualization are two of the charges most frequently levelled at Butler's work.

THE SUBJECT/GENDER

When it was first published in 1990, *Gender Trouble*'s deconstruction of the subject constituted a significant intervention into debates concerning identity and identity politics. Although the book was 'taken up' by readers who discerned political potential in its destabilization of identity categories, other critics and theorists have reacted against what they regard as the book's dangerous and nihilistic 'killing off' of the subject (see Chapter 2 of this book). You will remember that political philosopher Benhabib is concerned by what she perceives as Butler's Nietzschean 'death of the subject' thesis, while sociologists Hood Williams and Cealy Harrison suspect that Butler is theorizing a new gender ontology founded on performativity; so, while Benhabib thinks that Butler is depriving feminism of its foundations (which is indeed part of her ongoing political project), Hood Williams and Cealy Harrison argue that she does so only in order to posit an alternative foundation – performativity.

If these two sets of theorists regard Butler's theorizations of performativity as foundational, feminist critic Moi describes *power* as Butler's first principle (1999: 47). While Butler's putative foundationalism, along with her undoubted Foucauldianism (i.e. her focus on the operations of power in the formation of the subject), have troubled some of her critics, others are disturbed by her Freudianism, or the 'uses' to which she puts Freudian theory (for example, see Hood Williams and Cealy Harrison 1998: 83, 85). Prosser also objects to Butler's use of Freud, and he rejects performativity as quite simply *wrong* on the grounds that there are transgendered individuals who aspire to non-performative, constative identities (1998: 32; see also Chapter 2, this volume).

The feminist philosopher, Nancy Fraser, also questions whether subject-formation need always be oppressive (Benhabib *et al.* 1995:

68). Like Benhabib, Fraser is worried by Butler's deconstruction of the subject and she claims that, for Butler, women's liberation is liberation from identity. The formation of the subject through violence and exclusion is crucial to Butler's theorizations of identity, and in her reply to Fraser she insists that speaking subjects come into existence through exclusion and repression (Benhabib *et al*. 1995: 139). As Butler repeatedly asserts, the deconstruction of the subject is not synonymous with its *destruction*, but involves enquiring into the processes of its construction, along with the political consequences of assuming that the subject is a prerequisite of theory (Benhabib *et al*. 1995: 36). As we know, Butler's arguments do not stop here, and her deconstruction of the 'matter' of sex has generated at least as much critical debate as her theorizations of gender.

THE BODY

Butler's formulations of materiality and the body are probably among her most contentious theories, and they continue to puzzle and/or trouble her readers (see Chapters 2 and 3). The theorist Barbara Epstein writes that '[t]he assertion that sexual difference is socially constructed strains belief', and she rejects Butler's arguments on the basis of what seems to her to be the self-evident fact that 'the vast majority of humans are born male or female' (Epstein 1995: 101). Terry Lovell accepts that sex and gender are constructed, but argues that they are *necessary* social constructions that cannot be dispensed with (Lovell 1995: 334), while Moi insists that the body is 'real' and 'substantial'. Rejecting 'the old cliché' that language and matter are indissoluble, Moi claims that Butler risks eliding 'the concrete, historical body that loves, suffers and dies' (1999: 51, 49).

Actually, this is *not* the body that Butler attempts to describe, although she would not dispute the existence of concrete bodies in concrete historical situations (this is precisely what she argues at the end of *Subjects*). All the same, like Moi, the philosopher Carrie Hull discerns serious political shortcomings in Butler's accounts of materiality, and she concludes her article in the journal, *Radical Philosophy*, by insisting that there *are* some things that are rooted in a sexed material reality: 'the creatures we call women do share some material ground even as they share some other ground with the creatures we call men' (Hull 1997: 33). Discerning a disjunction between Butler's

Hegelian, idealistic roots and her rejection of materialism (which is possibly an idealistic move), Hull asserts that rejecting materialism precludes a political analysis of the workings of capitalism, society and economics, since again such theorizations are insufficient to address what Hull calls 'the real basis of suffering' (1997: 32).

Like Moi, Hull insists that there are different '"modalities" of materiality', but she does not go into detail as to what these are, nor does she specify *how* it is possible to make positive statements about the material body without engaging in violence and exclusion. Moreover, it is not entirely accurate to claim that Butler rejects materiality or materialism, since in the Preface to *Bodies* she goes out of her way to reassure the reader that she does accept the reality of 'primary and irrefutable experiences' such as eating and sleeping, pleasure and pain (BTM: xi). That Butler worries so extensively and consistently about exclusionary violence implies that she is by no means unaware of its consequences, i.e. the suffering it entails, but still it is possible to see how her theories might be construed as demoting suffering by paying little attention to interiority and 'experience'.

This is how Prosser has interpreted Butler's emphasis on recognition and the visual in her theorizations of sex in *Gender Trouble* and *Bodies*, and he points out that Butler's theoretical deliteralization of sex as the projection of a surface relies on a misreading and miscitation of Freud's *The Ego and The Id*. (In *Gender Trouble* and *Bodies* Butler argues, via Freud, that the body is a psychic effect and the projection of the ego, but in *The Ego and the Id* Freud claims that the ego is a bodily effect by arguing that the ego is a mental projection of the surface of the body that is derived from bodily sensations (Prosser 1998: 41).) Just as Hull argues that Butler cannot theorize suffering or economic oppression without recourse to materialism, Prosser relocates 'experience' as the ground of gendered and sexed identities. And yet Butler by no means denies the existence of 'experience' or suffering, even though it is true that much of her work is engaged in deconstructing ontological 'grounds' (such as the postulation 'I feel/experience, therefore I am') in order to reveal their groundlessness. Butler's deconstructions of matter might risk eliding pain and suffering but her focus on signification is deliberate, since it may contain subversive possibilities for the *re*signification of sex and gender.

LANGUAGE

In 'Why Butler?' I quoted a section from *Subjects* in which Butler acknowledges the difficulty of reading Hegel (SD: 19) and I warned you that the description might also seem applicable to Butler's *own* prose style, which has become notorious for what are widely deemed to be its obscurity, allusiveness and incoherence. Hopefully, you were not put off by this description, since I also pointed out that Butler's sentences strategically act upon the reader so that *what* is being said complements *how* it is being said. Far from prose style as 'bullying' as one critic has characterized it, this is prose style as dialectic, an active, indeed a *performative*, mode of writing that exemplifies performativity itself.

If Butler's prose style is performative, it would make little sense for her to theorize the incoherent, incomplete, unstable subject in sentences that present themselves as lucid, finished and epistemologically 'solid'. This is not how a number of Butler's readers have approached the issue of her prose style, which does at times seem to fit her own description of Hegel's 'confused, unwieldy and unnecessarily dense' sentences. Perhaps the most sustained set of objections come from the philosopher Martha Nussbaum in her article 'The Professor of Parody' (1999), in which Butler is taken to task for what Nussbaum calls the 'thick soup' of her prose – its allusiveness, density and inconclusiveness. (For a reading of Nussbaum's work, see Eaglestone 1997: 36–60.) In fact, it is Nussbaum who uses the epithet 'bullied' to describe readers who are awed by the wide range of philosophers and theories to which Butler alludes without explaining who or what they are or how they are being deployed. Nussbaum's attack (which is 'bullying' in its own way) makes three main points about Butler's language and her theorizations of language: 1) Butler's prose style is élitist, allusive and authoritarian; 2) what Nussbaum calls 'feminist thinkers of the new symbolic type' reduce materiality – particularly suffering and oppression – to what such feminists regard as 'an insufficiency of signs'; and 3) language is *not* equivalent to political action, and believing that it is results in political quietism and a collaboration with evil (Nussbaum 1999).

Nussbaum is not just objecting to Butler's mode of writing, but she also rejects the keystones of Butler's theory – performativity, citationality and parody, along with the deconstruction of 'matter' –

because of their focus on the symbolic. '[P]arodic performance is not so bad when you are a powerful tenured academic in a liberal university', Nussbaum argues; '[b]ut here is where Butler's focus on the symbolic, her proud neglect of the material side of life, becomes a fatal blindness. For women who are hungry, illiterate, disenfranchised, beaten, raped, it is not sexy or liberating to reenact, however parodically, the conditions of hunger, illiteracy, disenfranchisement, beating and rape. Such women prefer food and the integrity of their bodies' (Nussbaum 1999). Nussbaum argues that American academics such as Butler have succumbed to 'the extremely French idea' that speaking seditiously constitutes significant political action, leading them to reject materiality in favour of a verbal and symbolic politics that is only tenuously connected to what Nussbaum calls 'the real situation of real women' (Nussbaum 1999).

Although Nussbaum rehearses a litany of oppression and the oppressed, these 'real women' in 'real' pain remain troublingly unspecified and there are no 'concrete' examples of the sort of interventions feminist philosophers working in American universities should make. Writing in Butler's defence, Spivak claims that the 'hungry', 'illiterate' women towards whom Nussbaum merely gestures frequently engage in the performative gender practices Butler describes in her work, and she counters the assertion that Butler's 'hip quietism . . . collaborates with evil' by arguing that Nussbaum's 'equally hip, US benevolence toward "other women" collaborates with exploitation' (For Spivak's reply see 'Martha C. Nussbaum and her critics: an exchange.')

Nussbaum's accusations may be violent (or as Spivak puts it, 'vicious'), but the fact that the critical debate over language has generated so much feeling is an indication of its importance. Fraser finds Butler's essay 'Contingent Foundations' 'deeply antihumanist' because of its self-distancing idiom and its lack of attention to the impact and political consequences of such a prose style (Benhabib *et al.* 1995: 67), and McNay concurs with Fraser, asserting that Butler's account of agency is formal, abstract and lacking what McNay calls 'a hermeneutic dimension' (although she is not just referring to Butler's prose style here) (McNay 1999: 178). Butler's style has also been attacked in the *New York Times*, and in 1999 she was awarded a prize for 'bad writing' by the (right-wing) academic journal *Philosophy and Literature*.

It would be strange if a Professor of Rhetoric whose work is so extensively concerned with language and signification were to overlook the significance of her own language, but Butler's frequent allusions to the way she writes confirm that her style is a conscious political strategy and not the arrogance or the 'proud neglect' of which she has been accused. In her reply to the *New York Times*' attack Butler asks why trenchant social criticisms are expressed through difficult and demanding language, and in answer she asserts that such writing interrogates the tacit presumptions of what currently passes for 'common sense' by provoking new ways of looking at a familiar world. In a recent interview Butler also questions so-called 'ordinary language', once again affirming that, by writing in a way that is not easily accessible, the critic destabilizes what are possibly the reader's most cherished assumptions. This, she claims, is how newness enters the world (here she is following Bhabha), as the painfulness of 'passing through' difficult language necessitates taking up a critical attitude towards the social world as it is currently constituted. Becoming a critical intellectual involves working hard on difficult texts that demand attention, concentration and possibly 'translation' on the part of the reader. This hermeneutic process will overturn the erroneous assumption that readers and writers share a common language (CTS: 734), requiring the 'careful reading' for which Butler calls in her second contribution to *Feminist Contentions* (Benhabib *et al.* 1995), along with the painstaking, 'ruminative' analysis that, following Nietzsche, she recommends in 'What Is Critique?' ('Rumination' is a mode of reading Butler borrows from Nietzsche to describe the slow, careful analysis that theory and philosophy require. See WIC: 5; and Nietzsche 1887: 10.)

Clearly, Butler regards language *itself* as a political arena and a strategy of subversion, and yet we have encountered Nussbaum's objections to those so-called feminist philosophers of the new symbolic type who think that it is sufficient to talk or to write about politics in order to be political. Is Butler's writing political or, by eliding (or ignoring) material 'realities' as her critics claim she does, is she effectively evading politics altogether?

POLITICS

If Martha Nussbaum writes vehemently on the subject of Butler and language, she is equally emphatic on the issue of Butler's politics. Of course, language and politics are connected, and many of Nussbaum's objections to Butler's politics (or what she perceives as her *lack* of political engagement) are similar to the points she makes about language. The word Nussbaum uses most frequently in this context is 'quietism', by which she means that Butler's theories either advocate or engender a passive acceptance of the status quo by asserting that existing discourses can only be reworked rather than evaded. According to Nussbaum, Butler's theorizations of power and agency give rise to minor, individualistic acts of protest, such as 'doing femaleness' by 'turn[ing] it around, pok[ing] fun at it, do[ing] it a little differently', as Nussbaum somewhat reductively puts it (1999). Nussbaum does not regard parody and drag as viable alternatives for certain classes of 'oppressed women', and she argues that Butler's rejection of 'universal normative notions' may have dangerous legal and social consequences. Such omissions leave a 'void' at the heart of a political project that is unable to account for why some forms of subversion (such as parody and drag) are 'good' while others (such as tax evasion) are not. Nussbaum herself is firmly normative in her approach: 'you cannot simply resist as you please' she asserts, 'for there are norms of fairness, decency, and dignity that entail that this is bad behaviour. But then we have to articulate those norms – and this Butler refuses to do' (1999).

Fraser discerns a similar lacuna at the heart of Butler's politics, which in her view lacks both a subject (Fraser's contention that Butler understands women's liberation as a liberation from identity) as well as eliding the normative judgements and emancipatory alternatives that Fraser claims are essential for a liberatory feminist politics. 'Feminists need both deconstruction *and* reconstruction', she argues, 'destabilization of meaning *and* projection of utopian hope' (Benhabib *et al.* 1995: 71). McNay claims that the displacement of constraining social norms is a negative model of agency and, like Nussbaum, she regards performativity as a primarily individualistic political practice that is inadequately historicized and contextualized. As an example, McNay points out that the resignification of the term 'queer' may rely on a complex set of social and economic changes that are overlooked by Butler, and she argues that it is important to contextualize resignification within wider socio-economic relations in order to understand agency as a set of embedded practices rather than as an abstract structural potential (McNay 1999: 183, 187, 190). Similarly, Bordo argues that Butler's theorizations of the body and gender are abstract and give little idea of the contexts and workings of subversive parody, so that, while Butler is keenly attuned to the workings of phallocentrism and heterosexism, her Derridean/Foucauldian 'agenda' leads her to emphasize and celebrate resistance without contextualizing it culturally or historically (Bordo 1993: 292–5).

It is certainly true that Butler's texts do not contain prescriptions for political practice, and readers seeking guidance as to *how* exactly they should deploy performative and parodic modes of gender, or *what* precisely are the best ways of resisting dominant norms, may be disappointed. However, as with her prose style, this is not an omission on Butler's part (or what Nussbaum would call 'quietism') but a deliberate strategy of resistance – specifically here, a strategic resistance to the demand to specify or to prescribe effective political practices. In a recent interview with Vikki Bell, Butler wryly explains why *Gender Trouble* does not conclude with 'five suggestions on how to proceed':

> I think what's really funny – and this probably seems really odd considering the level of abstraction at which I work – is that I actually believe that politics has a character of contingency and context to it that cannot be predicted at the level of theory. And that when theory starts becoming programmatic, such as 'here are my five prescriptions', and I set up my typology, and my final chapter is called 'What is to be Done?', it pre-empts the whole problem of context and contingency, and I do think that political decisions are made in that lived moment and they can't be predicted from the level of theory.
>
> (Bell 1999b: 166–7)

It may indeed seem 'odd' for a theorist who has so extensively theorized performativity as that aspect of discourse that has the power to enact what it names, to downplay the political performativity of her own writing, and yet Butler's assertions are consistent with her emphasis on the political value of contingency and the importance of recognizing that 'event' and 'context' cannot be fully determined in advance. Accordingly, in the interview cited above Butler acknowledges herself as 'an ironic utopian', a self-interpellation that implies her commitment to suggesting alternatives to existing political configurations even while she recognizes that those alternatives are unstable and contingent (Bell 1999b: 167).

That Butler understands her work as ironic, implicated in past and future and therefore never self-present (a characterization resembling her descriptions of the ontological subject) does not mean that it is apolitical or disengaged, and there is a certain honesty in her admission of the disjunction between theory and politics and her awareness of the political limits of theory. Moreover, 'quietism' does not accurately describe theories that are engaged in a consistent and active interrogation of existing norms and discursive structures. Even though Butler identifies the normative direction or aspiration in her work, it is clear that she invokes such norms in the recognition of their contingency and instability. If Butler's political theories seem 'individualistic', as Nussbaum asserts, this is because the acts of voluntary insubordination she describes cannot take place within a totalizing frame of universal political prescriptivism that would merely replace one hegemonic structure with another, thereby forestalling the open political culture of contestation that Butler regards as a prerequisite of democracy and democratic change (CHU: 161).

LITERATURE

Although Butler only occasionally engages in literary criticism (for example in the early article on Wallace Stevens (NTI) and in *Bodies That Matter*), usually to underscore a political or philosophical point, her ideas have been influential in literary studies. In a collection of essays entitled *New Feminist Discourses*, Carol Watts argues that Butler's notion of gender as a cultural choice is useful for feminist literary analysis, since it provides a model for thinking about literature as the cultural site of gender construction (Watts 1992: 83). One such reading is Jaime Hovey's interpretation of Virginia Woolf's novel *Orlando* (1928). Hovey analyzes the representation of gendered, sexed and raced identities as masquerade (Hovey 1997: 396–7) and, although she simplifies performativity as performance, her reading exemplifies how Butler's ideas may assist in the interpretation of fictional texts that represent subject-formation and self-construction. So, in his contribution to *Novel-Gazing*, Jonathan Goldberg acknowledges the importance of Butler's and Sedgwick's readings of Willa Cather's novels as narratives of sexual knowledge (Goldberg 1997), while Tilottama Rajan analyzes the representation of desire in Mary Hays' nineteenth-century novel *Memoirs of Emma Courtney* through a Butlerian, Hegelian lens (Rajan 1993).

Finally, Butler's critiques of the exclusionary nature of identity categories are useful in the analysis of the construction of feminist literary studies. Mary Eagleton sees the writing of women's literary history as a problem of supplementarity, and her assertion that inclusive new histories expose the limits and exclusions of the old ones draws on Butler's theorizations of identity and/as exclusion (Eagleton 1996: 16).

DYNAMIC CONCLUSIONS

At the beginning of this chapter, I argued that the title 'After Butler' is somewhat pre-emptive, given that she is still actively involved in political and philosophical debates while continuing with her own writing and research. Forthcoming works include an edited book on bodies in theory, a dialogue with Bhabha on subjection, an article on ethics and sexual difference, and a piece on gender as translation in Willa Cather's *On the Gull's Road*. (See Yeghiayan 2001.) As she reminds her co-theorist Ernesto Laclau in her final contribution to *Contingency*, 'Dynamic Conclusions', Butler has by no means 'fallen asleep on the job', and she remains vigilantly, deconstructively aware of the strategic deployment of political signifiers and discourses that may be allowed to 'congeal at the moment of use' only to be uncongealed and further destabilized in other contexts (CHU: 269–70). What this means in practice is that Butler's work continues to exemplify the 'politics of discomfort', which she identifies as a crucial feature of Foucault's work, not in order to irritate or alienate her readers but so that existing norms and taken-for-granted assumptions may be questioned and genealogized.

Driving norms and universals into productive crisis may not make Butler popular in certain areas of the academy, and yet she remains committed to posing difficult questions in 'difficult' writing in order to challenge parochial assumptions and to create possibilities for radical difference:

> For me, there's more hope in the world when we can question what is taken for granted, especially about what it is to be a human ... What qualifies as a human, as a human subject, as human speech, as human desire? How do we circumscribe human speech or desire? At what cost? And at what cost to whom? These are questions that I think are important and that function within everyday grammar, everyday language, as taken-for-granted notions. We feel that we know the answers ...

(CTS: 764–5)

This book has not attempted to supply 'answers' to Butler or to any of the questions she poses in her work, and, if nothing else, it has hopefully opened up some new, perhaps radical ways of thinking about difference, even if it involves subjecting oneself to the anxiety and discomfort Butler identifies as a crucial part of the process of critical thinking.

FURTHER READING

For a complete list of works by and on Butler, see Eddie Yeghiayan's excellent and exhaustive bibliography on:

http://sun3.lib.uci.edu/indiv/scctr/Wellek/butler/html (accessed on 23 January 2001).

The sections below contain details of Butler's most important works and others that are relevant to this book. In addition, the annotated '"Essential" Theoretical Reading' section includes many of the sources from which Butler draws.

WORKS BY JUDITH BUTLER

BOOKS

—— (1987; reprint 1999) *Subjects of Desire: Hegelian Reflections in Twentieth-Century France*, New York: Columbia University Press.

Butler's first book on twentieth-century French philosophers' readings of Hegel is worth reading even if you're not familiar with Hegel, Sartre *et al*. Read the first chapter, 'Desire, Rhetoric and Recognition in Hegel's *Phenomenology of Spirit*' and the fourth, 'The Life and Death Struggles of Desire: Hegel and Contemporary French Theory' to get an idea of Hegel and his French readers. The Preface to the 1999 reprint is very useful too.

—— (1990; Anniversary edition 1999) *Gender Trouble: Feminism and the Subversion of Identity*, New York: Routledge.

It's important that you read this all the way through, but if you really don't have time, you could read at least section one of the first chapter, sections three and five of the second chapter, and section four of the third chapter. These sections discuss sex/gender/desire; melancholia; power, prohibition, agency; parodic subversion; and performativity. Make sure you look at the Preface to the tenth anniversary reprint as well.

—— (1993) *Bodies That Matter: On the Discursive Limits of 'Sex'*, New York: Routledge.

Butler's book on the discursive construction of 'sex' continues a number of arguments formulated in *Gender Trouble*. Notwithstanding the lesbian phallus (which you'll find in the second chapter), the first and eighth chapters ('Bodies that Matter' and 'Critically Queer') are crucial if you can't read the whole book. The Introduction is useful too.

—— (1997) *Excitable Speech: A Politics of the Performative*, New York: Routledge.

Butler's discussion of hateful language and representation isn't very long, and it's one of her more 'accessible' books. The chapters can be read as discrete essays, so you could choose any of them depending on your interests, but the first, 'On Linguistic Vulnerability' contains important theorizations of utterance via Austin, Althusser and others.

—— (1997) *The Psychic Life of Power: Theories in Subjection*, Stanford: Stanford University Press.

Reading psychoanalysis through Foucault, and Foucault through psychoanalysis, Butler gives useful re-readings of both. There's more Hegel in the first chapter, followed by Freud, Foucault, Nietzsche and Althusser. The fourth chapter, '"Conscience Doth Make Subjects of Us All": Althusser's Subjection', returns to the Althusserian man-on-the-street scenario, while the sixth, 'Psychic Inceptions: Melancholy, Ambivalence, Rage', contains further theorizations of melancholy.

—— (2000) *Antigone's Claim: Kinship Between Life and Death*, New York: Columbia University Press.

A slender book containing three lectures in which Butler discusses kinship structures within heterosexual hegemony. You don't need to be familiar with Sophocles' play to make sense of her arguments, and the third lecture, 'Promiscuous Obedience', contains Butler's observations on contemporary kinship structures and 'radical kinship' alternatives.

CO-AUTHORED BOOKS

Benhabib, Seyla, Judith Butler, Drucilla Cornell and Nancy Fraser (1995) *Feminist Contentions: A Philosophical Exchange*, London: Routledge.

Butler, Judith, Ernesto Laclau and Slavoj Žižek (2000) *Contingency, Hegemony, Universality: Contemporary Dialogues on the Left*, London: Verso.

Butler, Judith, John Guillory and Kendall Thomas (2000) *What's Left of Theory? New Work on the Politics of Literary Theory*, London: Routledge.

ARTICLES

—— (1986) 'Sex and Gender in Simone de Beauvoir's *Second Sex*', in *Yale French Studies* 72: 35–41, New Haven: Yale University Press.

This article and the following one are more or less identical, and they contain early formulations of gender as process, construct and dialectic. Read either of them.

—— (1987) 'Variations on Sex and Gender: Beauvoir, Wittig and Foucault', in Seyla Benhabib and Drucilla Cornell (eds) *Feminism as Critique: Essays on the Politics of Gender in Late-Capitalist Societies*, Cambridge: Polity Press, pp. 129–42.

—— (1989) 'Foucault and the Paradox of Bodily Inscriptions', *Journal of Philosophy* 86 (11): 601–7.

An important early article that contains 'in embryo' (as it were) many of the formulations of sex and gender Butler develops in *Gender Trouble*, *Bodies* and other later works.

—— (1989) 'Sexual Ideology and Phenomenological Description: A Feminist Critique of Merleau-Ponty's *Phenomenology of Perception*', in Jeffner Allen and Iris Marion Young (eds) *The Thinking Muse: Feminism and Modern French Philosophy*, Bloomington: Indiana University Press, pp. 85–100.

—— (1990) 'The Force of Fantasy: Mapplethorpe, Feminism, and Discursive Excess', *differences: A Journal of Feminist Cultural Studies* 2 (2): 105–25.

Butler on censorship. Some deft arguments exposing the weaknesses and anomalies of anti-pornography campaigns.

—— (1990) 'Gender Trouble, Feminist Theory, and Psychoanalytic Discourse', in Linda J. Nicholson (ed.) *Feminism/Postmodernism*, London: Routledge, pp. 324–40.

—— (1990) 'Imitation and Gender Insubordination', in Diana Fuss (ed.) *Inside Out: Lesbian Theories, Gay Theories*, London: Routledge, pp. 13–31.

—— (1991) 'The Nothing That Is: Wallace Stevens' Hegelian Affinities', in Bainard Cowan and Joseph G. Kronick (eds) *Theorizing American Literature: Hegel, the Sign, and History*, Baton Rouge: Louisiana State University Press, pp. 269–87.

For anyone interested in Hegel – oh, and the poet Wallace Stevens.

—— (1992) 'Contingent Foundations: Feminism and the Question of Postmodernism', in Judith Butler and Joan Scott (eds) *Feminists Theorize the Political*, London: Routledge, pp. 3–21.

An important article in which Butler theorizes postmodernism, feminism and 'the subject' in the context of the Gulf War.

—— (1992) 'Gender', in Elizabeth Wright (ed.) *Feminism and Psychoanalysis: A Critical Dictionary*, Oxford: Blackwell, pp. 140–5.

Useful and succinct if you're in a hurry to grasp the basics.

—— (1993) 'Endangered/Endangering: Schematic Racism and White Paranoia', in Robert Gooding Williams (ed.) *Reading Rodney King/Reading Urban Uprising*, New York: Routledge, pp. 15–22.

Butler on 'race' in the field of vision in the context of the trial of Rodney King's attackers. Some of the arguments in this article anticipate *Excitable Speech*.

—— (1994) 'Against Proper Objects', *differences: A Journal of Feminist Cultural Studies* 6 (2), (3): 1–26.

Butler argues against the 'territorialization' of queer theory, gay and lesbian studies and feminist theory. A challenging read.

—— (1995) 'For a Careful Reading', in Seyla Benhabib, Judith Butler, Drucilla Cornell and Nancy Fraser (co-authors) *Feminist Contentions: A Philosophical Exchange*, London: Routledge, pp. 127–43.

Butler's reply to her critics contains some useful descriptions of performativity.

—— (1996) 'Sexual Inversions', in Susan J. Hekman (ed.) *Feminist Interpretations of Michel Foucault*, Philadelphia: Pennsylvania University Press, pp. 344–61.

A timely re-reading of Foucault in which Butler argues passionately that death is a discursive industry in an age of epidemic where homosexuals are pathologized and medical technological advances are not readily available to people with Aids.

—— (1996) 'Universality in Culture', in Joshua Cohen (ed.) *For Love of Country: Debating the Limits of Patriotism: Martha C. Nussbaum with Respondents*, Boston: Beacon Press, pp. 43–52.

Butler contests universals and affirms the need to undertake the difficult work of cultural translation. Similar to her work in *Contingency, Hegemony, Universality*, but much shorter.

—— (1997) 'Performative Acts and Gender Constitution: An Essay on Phenomenology and Feminist Theory', in Katie Conboy, Nadia Medina and Sarah Stanbury (eds) *Writing on the Body: Female Embodiment and Feminist Theory*, New York: Columbia University Press, pp. 401–17. (Also in Sue-Ellen Case (ed.) *Performing Feminisms. Feminist Critical Theory and Theatre*, Baltimore: Johns Hopkins University Press, 1990.)

—— (1999) 'Revisiting Bodies and Pleasures', *Theory, Culture and Society* 16 (2): 11–20.

Butler argues against breaking with sex and desire in the rush to embrace bodies and pleasures that Foucault advocates in *The History of Sexuality Vol. 1*. As in 'Against Proper Objects', she also expresses reservations about some of queer theory's agendas.

—— (2000) 'Restaging the Universal: Hegemony and the Limits of Formalism'; 'Competing Universalities'; 'Dynamic Conclusions', in Judith Butler, Ernesto Laclau and Slavoj Žižek (co-authors) *Contingency, Hegemony, Universality: Contemporary Dialogues on the Left*, London: Verso, pp. 11–43, 136–81, 263–80.

Butler's three contributions critique universals and norms while affirming the value of contingency as a political strategy. Butler addresses the following questions: the compatibility of psychoanalysis and politics in general and Lacanianism and hegemony in particular; the future of feminism; the possibility of agency; the role of

Kantianism, universalism and historicism in the theoretical field; and the necessity of autocritique for the critical theorist.

—— (2001) 'What is Critique? An Essay on Foucault's Virtue', in David Ingram (ed.) *The Political: Readings in Continental Philosophy*, London: Basil Blackwell.

Butler's self-styled 'essay' on self-stylization as a form of critique asks who will count as a subject and what will count as life. This lecture is clear and to the point, and it forms a useful retrospective to earlier work. It also makes clear why Butler asks so many questions.

INTERVIEWS

—— (1992) 'The Body You Want: Liz Kotz Interviews Judith Butler', *Artforum International*, 3 Nov., (XXXI): 82–9.

Read this if you can get hold of it. Butler sounds relaxed and chatty, and she gives some nice sound-bites ('I don't believe that gender, race, or sexuality have to be identities. I think that they're vectors of power.' 'I'm a little tired of being queer . . . and of course I am totally queer as it were.')

—— (1994) 'Gender as Performance: An Interview with Judith Butler', *Radical Philosophy: A Journal of Socialist and Feminist Philosophy* 67 (Summer): 32–9. (Also in Peter Osborne (ed.) *A Critical Sense. Interviews with Intellectuals*, London: Routledge, 1996, pp. 109–25.)

This interview took place in the wake of *Gender Trouble* and *Bodies*, and among other subjects Butler discusses performance, performativity, psychoanalysis, 'race' and the lesbian phallus. Useful and accessible.

—— (1999) 'On Speech, Race and Melancholia: An Interview with Judith Butler', *Theory, Culture and Society* 16 (2): 163–74.

The focus here is on psychoanalysis, but Butler also discusses 'race', 'racialization' and melancholia.

—— (1999) 'A Bad Writer Bites Back', *New York Times*, 20 March. Accessed on 31 October 2000.

Pithy and to the point.

—— (2000) 'Politics, Power and Ethics: A Discussion Between Judith Butler and William Connolly', *Theory and Event* 4 (2). Online. Available at: http://euterpe-muse.press.jhu.edu/journals/theory_and_event/v0 04/4.2butler.html

This piece is theoretically challenging, and it contains interesting discussions of ethics, universality and dialectic, all of which Butler interrogates or critiques.

—— (2000) 'Changing the Subject: Judith Butler's Politics of Radical Resignification', Gary Olson and Lynn Worsham, *JAC* 20 (4).

A very useful recent interview which includes Butler's measured responses to criticisms of her style.

'ESSENTIAL' THEORETICAL READING

Althusser, Louis [1969] 'Ideology and Ideological State Apparatuses', in *Lenin and Philosophy and Other Essays*, trans. Ben Brewster, London: New Left Books, 1971.

Although Butler critiques Althusser in *Excitable* and *Psychic*, interpellation is crucial to her theorizations of subject-formation. Read the whole essay: it's not too long and not too difficult.

Austin, J.L. [1955] *How To Do Things With Words*, Cambridge, Mass.: Harvard University Press, 1962.

Short and accessible: vital for understanding how Butler deploys linguistic performativity in the contexts of Althusser and psychoanalysis.

de Beauvoir, Simone [1949] *The Second Sex* (*La Deuxième Sexe*), trans. H.M. Parshley, London: Everyman, 1993.

Don't be put off by the length of this book: sections IV and V are probably the most useful for understanding Butler, so you could skip straight to those. You'll find 'One is not born, but rather becomes, a woman' at the beginning of the twelfth chapter.

Derrida, Jacques [1972] 'Signature Event Context' ('Signature Evénement Contexte'), trans. A. Bass in Peggy Kamuf (ed.) *A Derrida Reader: Between the Blinds*, New York: Columbia University Press, 1991.

Derrida's short, not very difficult essay informs Butler's theorizations of citationality from *Bodies* onwards. In his delimitations of authorial intention, context and meaning, Derrida is responding to Austin's emphasis on context and convention, but, unlike Austin, Derrida emphasizes the 'citationality, duplication, duplicity . . . iterability of the mark'.

Foucault, Michel [1976] *The History of Sexuality Vol. I: La Volonté de Savoir*, trans. Robert Hurley, London: Penguin, 1990.

Widely regarded as one of the 'founding' texts of queer theory, *The History of Sexuality* traces the discursive production of sex in bourgeois, capitalist, European societies. Foucault argues that sex has been put into discourse since the end of the sixteenth century, when the repression of sex coincided with what he calls 'a veritable discursive explosion' of sexual discourses. Indispensable, accessible and short, Butler draws from this text throughout her work, and in her article 'Sexual Inversions' she reconsiders Foucault's arguments in the context of Aids.

Freud, Sigmund [1917] 'Mourning and Melancholia' ('Trauer und Melancholie'), in Angela Richards (ed.) *The Pelican Freud Library Vol. 11*, London: Penguin, 1984.

Short, accessible, and crucial to understanding Butler's formulations of melancholic sexed and gendered identities.

—— [1923] *The Ego and the Id* (*Das Ich und das Es*), in Angela Richards (ed.) *The Pelican Freud Library Vol. 11*, London: Penguin, 1984.

This essay is not quite so short and not quite so accessible, but it is indispensable nonetheless, and worth the effort. Freud now describes all ego formation as a melancholic structure and a repository of prohibited desires, and he argues that it is on this basis that gender/sexed identities are formed. Butler disagrees with Freud that the infant's desire is determined by its primary disposition and she argues that sexual dispositions are products of the law.

Hegel, G.W.F. [1807] *Phenomenology of Spirit* (*Phänomenologie des Geistes*), trans. A.V. Miller, Oxford: Oxford University Press, 1979.

Well worth at least a try, and if you don't have the stamina to read the whole thing, skip to section IV (A) and (B), 'Independence and Dependence of Self-consciousness: Lordship and Bondage' and 'Freedom of Self-consciousness: Stoicism, Scepticism, and the Unhappy Consciousness', where Hegel describes the encounter between the lord and his bondsman and its aftermath. If you get stuck, refer to Peter Singer or Jonathan Rée, both of whom provide excellent, brief introductions to Hegel (see below).

Kristeva, Julia [1980] *Powers of Horror: An Essay on Abjection* (*Pouvoirs de l'Horreur. Essai sur l'Abjection*), trans. Leon S. Roudiez, New York: Columbia University Press, 1982.

Abjection, what is rejected and expelled by/from the subject, is another keystone of *Gender Trouble*. Kristeva writes that '[i]t is . . . not lack of cleanliness or health that causes abjection but what disturbs identity, system, order. What does not respect borders, positions, rules. The in-between, the ambiguous, the composite'. According to Butler, for the heterosexual it is the homosexual that is the abjected 'Other', but her brilliant application of psychoanalytic theory makes the abject central to the straight subject. Read the first chapter, 'Approaching Abjection'.

Lacan, Jacques (1977) *Écrits: A Selection*, London: Routledge.

People are always talking about how difficult Lacan is, but if you've read Butler you shouldn't have a problem with this. 'The Mirror Stage as Formative of the Function of the I as Revealed in Psychoanalytic Experience' and 'The Signification of the Phallus' are the most important essays for the purposes of understanding Butler. The notion that 'I' is a spatial, topographical structure will be familiar to you in the first essay, as will what Lacan calls 'the signifying function of the phallus' in the second essay.

MacKinnon, Catharine A. (1993) *Only Words*, Cambridge, Mass.: Harvard University Press.

MacKinnon's passionate indictment of a legal system that safeguards pornography, racial and sexual harassment as 'protected' speech under the First Amendment to the US Constitution. Important, short and accessible.

Nietzsche, Friedrich [1887] *On the Genealogy of Morals (Zur Genealogie der Moral)*, trans. Douglas Smith, Oxford: Oxford University Press, 1998.

An important text in which you'll find Nietzsche's discussions of slave morality, *ressentiment*, suffering, guilt and asceticism. If you're looking for 'there is no being behind doing', and so on, you'll find it in section thirteen of the first essay.

Rée, Jonathan (1987) *Philosophical Tales: An Essay on Philosophy and Literature*, London: Methuen.

Not exactly 'essential theory', but Rée's useful (and short) book contains an excellent chapter on Hegel with a section on *Phenomenology*, complete with a diagram of the Spirit's 'journey' towards absolute knowledge. Read the third chapter, 'Hegel's Vision.'

Rubin, Gayle (1975) 'The Traffic in Women: Notes on the "Political Economy" of Sex', in Rayna R. Reiter (ed.) *Towards An Anthropology of Women*, New York: Monthly Review Press.

Rubin's feminist anthropological analyses of 'the sex/gender system' as a set of socially imposed arrangements and divisions remain an important influence for Butler's work. It's easy to see why, when Rubin makes statements such as 'Gender is a socially imposed division of the sexes'.

Singer, Peter (1983) *Hegel*, Oxford: Oxford University Press.

A useful, succinct introduction to Hegel's ideas.

Wittig, Monique (1992) *The Straight Mind and Other Essays*, Boston: Beacon Press.

Butler departs from Wittig on many points, but Wittig's 'materialist lesbian' writings nonetheless remain a crucial influence for her. Read at least the first three essays in this collection ('The Category of Sex', 'One Is Not Born a Woman' and 'The Straight Mind'), along with 'The Mark of Gender', where, like Butler, Wittig argues that sex and gender are not 'natural' a prioris.

WORKS CITED

Note: Works by Judith Butler that are cited in this book are listed in the Further Reading section, pp. 153–62.

Althusser, Louis [1969] 'Ideology and Ideological State Apparatuses', in *Lenin and Philosophy and Other Essays*, trans. Ben Brewster, London: New Left Books, 1971, pp. 123–73.

Austin, J.L. [1955] *How To Do Things With Words*, Cambridge, Mass.: Harvard University Press, 1962.

Barbin, Herculine (1980) *Herculine Barbin. Being the Recently Discovered Journals of a Nineteenth-century French Hermaphrodite*, trans. Richard McDougall, introduced by Michel Foucault, Brighton: The Harvester Press Ltd.

Bell, Vikki (1999a) 'Mimesis as Cultural Survival: Judith Butler and Anti-Semitism', *Theory, Culture and Society* 16 (2): 133–61.

—— (1999b) 'On Speech, Race and Melancholia. An Interview with Judith Butler', *Theory, Culture and Society*, 16 (2): 163–74.

Benhabib, Seyla, Judith Butler, Drucilla Cornell and Nancy Fraser (1995) *Feminist Contentions: A Philosophical Exchange*, London: Routledge.

Bhabha, Homi (1994) *The Location of Culture*, London: Routledge.

Bordo, Susan (1993) *Unbearable Weight: Feminism, Western Culture, and the Body*, Berkeley: California University Press.

Bourdieu, Pierre [1980] *The Logic of Practice (Le Sens Pratique)*, trans. Richard Nice, Cambridge: Polity Press, 1990.

—— (1991) *Language and Symbolic Power*, trans. Gino Raymond and Matthew Adamson, John B. Thompson (ed.), Cambridge: Polity Press.

de Beauvoir, Simone [1949] *The Second Sex (La Deuxième Sex)*, trans. H.M. Parshley, London: Everyman, 1993.

de Lauretis, Teresa (1987) *Technologies of Gender: Essays on Film, Theory and Fiction*, Bloomington: Indiana University Press.

Derrida, Jacques [1968] 'The Pit and the Pyramid: An Introduction to Hegel's Semiology', trans. A. Bass, in *Margins of Philosophy*, Brighton: Harvester, 1982, pp. 69–108.

—— [1972] 'Signature Event Context' ('Signature Evénement Contexte'), in Peggy Kamuf (ed.) *A Derrida Reader: Between the Blinds*, New York: Columbia University Press, 1999, pp. 80–111.

Dollimore, Jonathan (1996) 'Bisexuality, Heterosexuality, and Wishful theory', *Textual Practice* 10 (3): 523–39.

Eaglestone, Robert (1997) *Ethical Criticism. Reading After Levinas*, Edinburgh: Edinburgh University Press.

Eagleton, Mary (1996) 'Who's Who and Where's Where: Constructing Feminist Literary Studies', *Feminist Review* 53: 1–23.

Eliot, T.S. [1932] *Sweeney Agonistes: Fragments of an Aristophanic Melodrama*, in *The Complete Poems and Plays of T.S. Eliot*, London: Faber, 1969, pp. 83–119.

Epstein, Barbara (1995) 'Why Post-Structuralism is a Dead End for Progressive Thought', *Socialist Review* 25 (2).

Eribon, Didier (1991) *Michel Foucault*, trans. Betsy Wing, Cambridge, Mass.: Harvard University Press.

Foucault, Michel [1961] *Madness and Civilisation: A History of Insanity in the Age of Reason (Histoire de la Folie)*, trans. Richard Howard 1971, London: Routledge, 1992.

—— [1971] 'Nietzsche, Genealogy, History' ('Nietzsche, Généalogie, Histoire'), in Paul Rabinow (ed.) *The Foucault Reader: An Introduction to Foucault's Thought*, London: Penguin, 1984, pp. 76–100.

—— [1975] *Discipline and Punish: The Birth of the Prison* (*Surveiller et Punir: Naissance de la Prison*), trans. Alan Sheridan, London: Penguin, 1977.

—— [1976] *The History of Sexuality Vol. I* (*La Volonté de Savoir*), trans. Robert Hurley, London: Penguin, 1990.

—— [1978] 'What Is Critique?', in Sylvère Lotringer and Lysa Hochroth (eds) *The Politics of Truth: Michel Foucault*, New York: Semiotexte, 1997.

Fraser, Nancy (1995) 'False Antitheses', in Seyla Benhabib, Judith Butler, Drucilla Cornell and Nancy Fraser (co-authors) *Feminist Contentions: A Philosophical Exchange*, London: Routledge, pp. 59–74.

Freud, Sigmund [1911] 'On the Mechanism of Paranoia', in *Sigmund Freud: Collected Papers Vol. 3*, trans. Alix and James Strachey, New York: Basic Books, 1959, pp. 444–66.

—— [1913] *Totem and Taboo: Some Points of Agreement between the Mental Lives of Savages and Neurotics* (*Totem und Tabu*), *The Pelican Freud Library Vol. 13*, London: Penguin, 1990, pp. 43–224.

—— [1914] 'On Narcissism: An Introduction' ('Zur Einführung des Narzismus'), *The Pelican Freud Library Vol. 11*, London: Penguin, 1991, pp. 59–97.

—— [1917] 'Mourning and Melancholia' ('Trauer und Melancholie'), *The Pelican Freud Library Vol. 11*, London: Penguin, 1991, pp. 245–68.

—— [1923] *The Ego and the Id* (*Das Ich und das Es*), *The Pelican Freud Library Vol. 11*, London: Penguin, 1991, pp. 339–407.

—— [1930] *Civilisation and Its Discontents* (*Das Unbehagen in der Kultur*), *The Pelican Freud Library Vol. 12*, London: Penguin, 1991, pp. 243–340.

Gates, Henry Louis Jr (1992) 'The Master's Pieces: On Canon-Formation and the African-American Tradition', in H.L. Gates (ed.) *Loose Canons: Notes on the Culture Wars*, Oxford: Oxford University Press, pp. 17–42.

Gilroy, Paul (1993) *The Black Atlantic: Modernity and Double Consciousness*, London: Verso.

Goldberg, Jonathan (1997) 'Strange Brothers', in Eve Sedgwick (ed.) *Novel-Gazing: Queer Readings in Fiction*, Durham and London: Duke University Press, pp. 465–82.

Hardy, Thomas [1891] Tess of the d'Urbervilles, David Skilton (ed.), London: Penguin, 1978.

Hegel, G.W.F. [1807] Phenomenology of Spirit (Phänomenologie des Geistes), trans. A.V. Miller, Oxford: Oxford University Press, 1979.

Hood Williams, John and Wendy Cealy Harrison (1998) 'Trouble With Gender', The Sociological Review 46 (1): 73–94.

hooks, bell (1996) 'Is Paris Burning?', in bell hooks Reel to Real: Race, Sex, and Class At the Movies, London: Routledge, pp. 214–26.

Hovey, Jaime (1997) '"Kissing a Negress in the Dark": Englishness as Masquerade in Woolf's Orlando', PMLA 112 (3): 393–404.

Hull, Carrie (1997) 'The Need in Thinking: Materiality in Theodor W. Adorno and Judith Butler', Radical Philosophy 84, July/August: 22–35.

Hyppolite, Jean [1946] Genesis and Structure of Hegel's 'Phenomenology of Spirit' (Genèse et Structure de la 'Phenomenologie de l'Esprit'), trans. Samuel Cherniak and John Heckman, Evanston: Northwestern University Press, 1974.

Inwood, Michael (1982) Hegel Dictionary, Oxford: Blackwell.

Kojève, Alexandre [1941] Introduction to the Reading of Hegel: Lectures on the Phenomenology of Spirit (Introduction à la Lecture de Hegel: Leçons sur la Phenomenologie de l'Esprit), trans. James H. Nichols Jr, New York: Basic Books, 1969.

Kristeva, Julia (1982) Powers of Horror: An Essay on Abjection (Pouvoirs de l'Horreur. Essai sur l'Abjection), trans. Leon S. Roudiez, New York: Columbia University Press.

Lacan, Jacques [1949] 'The Mirror Stage as Formative of the Function of the I as Revealed in Psychoanalytic Experience', in Jacques Lacan Écrits: A Selection, London: Routledge, 1977; reissued 2001, pp. 1–7.

—— [1958] 'The Signification of the Phallus', in Jacques Lacan Écrits: A Selection, London: Routledge, 1977; reissued 2001, pp. 281–91.

Larsen, Nella (1928, 1929) Quicksand and Passing, Deborah E. MacDowell (ed.), New Brunswick, New Jersey: Rutgers University Press, 1986.

Lovell, Terry (1996) 'Feminist Social Theory', in Brian S. Turner (ed.) The Blackwell Companion to Social Theory, Oxford: Blackwell, pp. 307–39.

MacKinnon, Catharine A. (1993) *Only Words*, Cambridge, Mass.: Harvard University Press.

McNay, Lois (1999) 'Subject, Psyche and Agency: The Work of Judith Butler', *Theory, Culture and Society* 16 (2): 175–93.

Moi, Toril (1999) *What Is a Woman? and Other Essays*, Oxford: Oxford University Press.

Nietzsche, Friedrich [1887] *On the Genealogy of Morals* (*Zur Genealogie der Moral*), trans. Douglas Smith, Oxford: Oxford University Press, 1996.

Nussbaum, Martha (1999) 'The Professor of Parody', *New Republic*, 22 February. Online. Available at: http://www.tnr.com/archive/0299/022299/nussbaum022299.html

O'Driscoll, Sally (1996) 'Outlaw Readings: Beyond Queer Theory', *Signs: Journal of Women in Culture and Society* 22 (1): 30–49.

Prosser, Jay (1998) *Second Skins: The Body Narratives of Transsexuality*, New York: Columbia University Press.

Rajan, Tilottama (1993) 'Autonarration and Genotext in Mary Hays' *Memoirs of Emma Courtney*', *Studies in Romanticism* 32: 149–76.

Rée, Jonathan (1987) *Philosophical Tales: An Essay on Philosophy and Literature*, London: Methuen.

Rubin, Gayle (1975) 'The Traffic in Women: Notes on the "Political Economy" of Sex', in Rayna R. Reiter (ed.) *Towards An Anthropology of Women*, New York: Monthly Review Press, pp. 157–210.

Sartre, Jean Paul [1943] *Being and Nothingness: An Essay in Phenomenological Ontology* (*L'Être et le Néant: Essai d'Ontologie Phénoménologique*), trans. Hazel E. Barnes, London: Methuen, 1977.

Saussure, Ferdinand de [1916] *Course in General Linguistics* (*Cours de Linguistique Générale*), trans. Roy Harris, London: Duckworth, 1983.

Sedgwick, Eve (1990) *Epistemology of the Closet*, London: Penguin.

—— (1994) *Tendencies*, London: Routledge.

Shildrick, Margrit (1996) 'Judith Butler', in Stuart Brown, Dina Collinson and Robert Wilkinson (eds) *Blackwells Biographical Dictionary of Twentieth-Century Philosophers*, Oxford: Blackwell, pp. 117–18.

Sinfield, Alan (1996) 'Diaspora and Hybridity: Queer Identities and the Ethnicity Model', *Textual Practice* 10 (2): 271–93.

Singer, Peter (1983) *Hegel*, Oxford: Oxford University Press.

Thurschwell, Pamela (2000) *Sigmund Freud*, London: Routledge.

Warner, Michael (1993) *Fear of a Queer Planet: Queer Politics and Social Theory*, Minneapolis: University of Minnesota Press.

Watts, Carol (1992) 'Releasing Possibility into Form: Cultural Choice and the Woman Writer', in Isobel Armstrong (ed.) *New Feminist Discourses: Critical Essays on Theories and Texts*, London: Routledge, pp. 83–102.

Wittig, Monique (1992) *The Straight Mind and Other Essays*, Boston: Beacon Press.

Elizabeth Wright (ed.) (1992) *Feminism and Psychoanalysis: A Critical Dictionary*, Oxford: Blackwell.

Yeghiayan, Eddie (2001) *Bibliography of Works By and On Judith Butler*. Online. Available at: http://sun3.lib.uci.edu/indiv/scctr/Wellek/butler/html (accessed on 23 January 2001).

INDEX

identification 52–3, 56, 58, 133

identity 2, 4, 10, 29, 73, 115, 119, 137, 141

ideology 6, 104

'Ideology and Ideological State Apparatuses', *see* Louis Althusser

illocutionary acts 88, 101–2; *see also* J.L. Austin

imaginary, the 38, 83, 87; *see also* Jacques Lacan

imitation 66

incest taboo 38, 53, 55, 56, 58, 60; generativity of 59

incorporation 54, 56, 58

individual, the 10

influence (Butler's) 2, 137–8, 140–2

internalization 55, 56, 64

International Gay and Lesbian Human Rights Commission 139

interpellation 75, 76, 77–80, 98, 99, 106–7, 115, 128–30, 135; *see also* Louis Althusser

intersexuality 70

Introduction to the Reading of Hegel, *see* Alexandre Kojève

introjection 53, 54, 57

Inwood, Michael 24, 25

Irigaray, Luce 6

'Is Paris Burning?', *see* bell hooks

iterability 114; *see also* recitation

Izzard, Eddie 96

Joyce, James, 23

Kant, Immanuel 20

Kierkegaard, Søren 20

King, Rodney 108

kinship 52

Kojève, Alexandre 29, 32, 33–4, 41

Kristeva, Julia 29, 39–40, 41, 61; *see also* abjection

Lacan, Jacques 6, 7, 20, 37–8, 41, 52, 60, 69, 82–5, 87, 88, 98

lack and loss 38, 119, 131, 135

Laclau, Ernesto 140, 151

language 14, 31, 36, 84, 86, 97, 99–117, 112, 115, 117, 145–7; *see also* style

Language and Symbolic Power, *see* Pierre Bourdieu

Larsen, Nella 76, 93–4

law 51, 59, 60, 64, 67, 79, 89, 99, 102, 103–10, 111, 116, 117, 119, 120, 122, 124–5, 127, 130, 135, 138

Lemmon, Jack 96

lesbian, as term 114, 115

lesbian phallus 82–3, 84–5, 86–7, 88; and race 94–5

lesbian/gay/bisexual theory 2, 9, 140

Lévi-Strauss, Claude 21, 52, 59

libido 125; *see also* desire

literature 139, 150–1

Livingston, Jennie 76, 94

Logic, *see* G.W.F. Hegel

The Logic of Practice, *see* Pierre Bourdieu

Loose Canons, *see* Henry Louis Gates Jr

lordship and bondage, *see* G.W.F. Hegel

loss, of Self 26

Lovell, Terry 143

MacKinnon, Catharine 105, 108, 109; *see also* pornography

Madness and Civilisation, *see* Michel Foucault

Mapplethorpe, Robert 103; *see also* 'The Force of Fantasy: Mapplethorpe, Feminism and Discursive Excess'

Übermensch, the 38
Understanding, the 13
unhappy consciousness 121–2
universality 139, 148, 150

vagina, the 79
'Variations on Sex and Gender: Beauvoir, Wittig, and Foucault' 8, 46, 48
Victor, Victoria, see Julie Andrews
violence 123–4, 134, 143

Warner, Michael 141
Watts, Carole 150
What Is A Woman?, see Toril Moi

'What Is Critique? An Essay on Foucault's Virtue' 6, 114, 130, 138–40, 147; *see also* Michel Foucault
What's Left of Theory? New Work on the Politics of Literary Theory 139
Williams, Robin 67
Wittig, Monique 6, 7, 48, 60
Woolf, Virginia, *see* Jamie Hovey
Wright, Elizabeth 127

Yeghiayan, Eddie 138, 151

Žižek, Slavoj 140